DEEPAK CHOPRA

fire
in the
Heart

A SPIRITUAL GUIDE
FOR TEENS

Simon Pulse
New York   London   Toronto   Sydney

SIMON PULSE
An imprint of Simon & Schuster Children's Publishing Division
1230 Avenue of the Americas, New York, NY 10020
Copyright © 2004 by Deepak Chopra
All rights reserved, including the right of reproduction in whole or
in part in any form.
SIMON PULSE and colophon are registered trademarks of Simon & Schuster, Inc.
Also available in a Simon & Schuster Books for Young Readers hardcover edition.
Designed by O'Lanso Gabbidon
The text of this book was set in Berkeley Book.
Manufactured in the United States of America
First Simon Pulse edition December 2006
10 9 8 7 6 5 4
The Library of Congress has cataloged the hardcover edition as follows:
Chopra, Deepak.
Fire in the heart : a spiritual guide for teens / Deepak Chopra.
p. cm.
Summary: By recounting his own experiences at age fifteen, Deepak Chopra, a noted Hindu author
and physician, provides a blueprint for teens who are seeking their own spiritual paths.
ISBN-13: 978-0-689-86216-8 (hc.)
ISBN-10: 0-689-86216-4 (hc.)
1. Spiritual life. 2. Teenagers. [1. Spiritual life. 2. Hinduism] I. Title.
BL624.C4767 2004
204'.4'0835—dc22
2003020174
ISBN-13: 978-0-689-86217-5 (pbk.)
ISBN-10: 0-689-86217-2 (pbk.)

To all the teenagers today and tomorrow upon
whom the fate of the world depends

Every child that is born is proof that God
has not yet given up on human beings.
—Rabindranath Tagore

Contents

Contents

Before You Begin . . .

A boy of fifteen is standing on a high green hill overlooking a valley. The valley is even more green and lush. It rolls away in wave after wave until the boy thinks it must never end.

"Do you see?" a voice says.

The boy turns, and next to him an old man is standing. The old man has a long white beard, and there is a gleam in his eye.

"Yes, I see," the boy says, but his heart is beating so fast he can hardly express himself.

"I want you to tell me what you see. I have to be sure you learned your lessons well," the old man says.

Ordinarily it would have broken the boy's heart to say good-bye, because he thought the old man with the white beard would be with him forever.

"I see that all this is mine," the boy says. "I belong to the universe, and it belongs to me." He stretches his arms out as if he could own it all—the high hill, the green valley, the whole span of years ahead of him. Somehow, even though it sounds impossible, he *does* own it all.

"Never forget this," the old man says. He presses his palms together and bows in respect, and the boy, bowing even deeper, does the same.

And that's the last I saw of him. Because I was the boy on the hill, and in four short days, the only time we were together, the old man changed my life. Each day he answered a question that you are going to read about in this book:

> *Do I have a soul?*
> *How do wishes come true?*
> *What is the supreme force in the universe?*
> *How can I change the world?*

These are big questions, and when I was young and bursting with idealism, they were burning questions. I didn't just want to know the answers—I *had* to know. There will always be burning questions in life, but these four remain special because they start a spark, and from that spark you will have a fire in your heart. That fire will make you live your life with excitement and passion.

The old man with the white beard showed me the spiritual side of life, where real passion and excitement come from. I'm going to tell you about our days together, down to the smallest detail, until you are given what I was given. Then you can be transformed too, wherever you are. So before you begin, take a deep breath. This story could turn out to be yours.

Day One

Do I Have a Soul?

Baba

When I was fifteen, my school was on a green hillside overlooking a valley even more green and lush. That part you already know. Every day I saw this beautiful view, except when the valley filled with billowing mist. On those mornings I walked to school with wisps of white curling around me, like walking through clouds. It was on just such a day, as I was making my way down the road, that a stranger's voice called out.

"Come," it said. "I've been waiting."

The voice seemed to come from another world. I imagine you've walked through fog and know how it creates a hush all around you, like a cocoon. Then my eye caught something. An old man was sitting under the biggest, most twisted tree by the side of the road.

"Baba, I'm on my way to school," I said. "You must be waiting for someone else." I grew up in India, and *baba* is a term of respect that is given to someone who is considered a wise or holy man.

"We need to talk," he said in a most definite voice. I drew closer. Baba was sitting on the ground with his legs crossed. His beard was almost as white as the immaculate cotton pants and shirt that he wore.

"You're old enough to know things now," he said, not waiting for me to reply. "And who else is going to tell you?"

I felt a shiver run down my spine. "What kind of things?" I asked.

"Invisible things. Secret things." Suddenly Baba laughed. "How mysterious do I have to sound for you to listen?"

I started to forget about school. All kinds of images were filling my mind. Sitting there in that cross-legged position, the old man looked like Buddha, who became enlightened sitting under a tree. His long white beard made Baba look wizardly, like Merlin, and the gleam in his eye told me unmistakably that he must be wise, like Socrates.

"I'm not asking much. Just give me one day," Baba coaxed.

Hesitantly I sat down beside him under the gnarled, twisted tree. The sun was burning the mist off now. Between billows of fog we could glimpse the green tea plantations that filled the valley and surrounding hills.

"This won't be like school," Baba said. "I'm going to teach you a new way to see and a new way to be."

He pointed at the scenery. "What do you see? I mean right now, at this very moment?"

"I see you and this tree, and I see the fog lifting from the valley," I said.

Baba leaned closer. "Want to know what I see? I see your soul." He was catching my attention more and more. "I see a world for you to possess. I see eternity." Baba stopped, and I felt another shiver. "Do you believe me?" he asked.

"I want to believe you, but I can't see any of those things," I said.

"Of course not. It takes a new way of seeing, which is why I had to find you," he said. "A few more years and you might be lost. The old ways are hard to break."

I was at that age when a dreamy inclination comes easily. In fact, the reason I hadn't noticed Baba was that I had been dreaming my way to school. Now it seemed as if I had conjured up a vision out of the mist.

The old man's eyes sharpened. "I'm not talking about fantasies and pink clouds," he said. "You need to know how reality works. Only what's real has power, even when it looks like magic."

"Okay," I said. I had the uncomfortable feeling that he had read my mind when I wondered if he was imaginary.

"In reality there *is* eternity everywhere," said Baba. "In reality your soul is here for you to experience it. I'll show you what I mean."

He reached down and took up a handful of sand from the side of the road. "Feel it," he said. "What's it like?"

He dropped some of the sand into my hands. "It's rough and sharp and grainy," I said. "And it's warm from the sun."

"Would it surprise you if I told you that none of that is real?" he asked.

I felt confused. "Of course it's real."

"But sand is made of molecules," said Baba. "And molecules aren't sharp or rough or grainy. I could take the molecules in sand and turn them into glass, which is completely smooth. Of course, molecules aren't real either."

"Why not?"

"Because they are made of atoms, and atoms are just blurry clouds of energy. You can't see or touch one, and isn't that how you measure real things, by seeing and touching them? Come to think of it, energy isn't real either."

By now I didn't feel like arguing; this was a completely new way of seeing things, just as he had promised.

"Energy vibrates everywhere in the universe," Baba said. "But it springs from the void, which is empty and still. You won't know what's real until we go there. Shall we?"

He let the sand sift through his fingers, and for a moment it was like watching someone letting the whole world sift through his fingers, the world I thought I lived in.

"This is very strange," I murmured.

"Ah, so the old ways are not looking quite so certain,"

he said, sounding pleased. "What will be left when everything solid vanishes before your eyes?"

"Nothing," I said.

"Nothing!" he repeated. "That's exactly right. But when we're through, nothing will turn into everything—your soul, God, an infinite world for you to possess. Shall we?" he asked again.

"Absolutely," I said.

WHAT I LEARNED

Spirituality is about a new way of seeing and a new way of being. When Baba told me that one thing, he told me all I had to know. It wasn't even necessary to use the word *spirituality*. Words are never as important as reality itself, and what's real is that you and I are like walking clouds at the atomic level. Atoms are a lot more empty than they are solid, which means that *we* are a lot more empty than we are solid (every person is more than 99.999999 percent empty space; the space between the earth and the sun is much smaller by comparison).

Just beneath the surface, where things look reassuring and solid, we all should fly apart and float away into a fog, but we don't. This is because we aren't really empty. There's an invisible *something* to be discovered inside us.

"A mysterious force is holding things together and making patterns out of clouds of energy," Baba told me. "You'd better find out what that force is."

"Why?" I asked.

"Because it's everywhere. It's finer than the finest atom. It's subtler than the subtlest energy. It's more real than anything you have ever seen. Don't even compare it to physical forces like gravity and electricity," he said. "Unless an invisible *something* existed, there would be no universe. And no you."

So that's how it started: A boy and an old man set out to hunt the invisible *something* that is real even when everything else vanishes. Only years later, after I was grown up, did I come across some lines that perfectly state what we were after. They come from the poet William Blake, and you could call them the motto for this book.

To see a world in a grain of sand
And a heaven in a wild flower,
Hold infinity in the palm of your hand
And eternity in an hour.

You Won't Believe Your Eyes

We'll never find anything invisible if you believe your eyes," said Baba. "Most people do that all the time. It's a bad habit." He pointed to a rock lying beside him on the ground. "Even though this is really an energy cloud, a rock looks very solid and heavy, doesn't it?"

"Yes, because it is. A cloud wouldn't hurt if you dropped one on your foot," I said.

"Ah, you do trust your five senses," said Baba. "Why shouldn't you? After all, the world is flat, just the way your eyes see it."

"Well, no, that's something I couldn't trust," I said.

"Oh, but the sun moves across the sky and sets in the west at night, doesn't it?" said Baba.

"No, it only looks that way," I admitted.

"So you're already in the habit of not trusting your eyes," said Baba, smiling a certain way. I came to call this his *I know a secret* smile, and one could never quite tell when it was coming.

"Maybe I can't trust my eyes all the time, but how can I rely on what I can't see at all?" I asked.

"Here's a clue wrapped in a story," said Baba. "One night while you were asleep, your body started talking to itself. The heart spoke up first. 'I'm sick of pumping blood all day for the stomach. Why should I? I should be working just for myself.'

"When it heard this, the stomach replied, 'You should talk. I digest food all day for the brain. It takes whatever I give, and frankly, I should be working just for myself too.'

"When the brain heard this, it said, 'I think all the time about what to put in the stomach. Do you realize how easily it gets upset? If anybody should be working just for themselves, it's me.'

"You can see why this argument is silly," said Baba. "In reality every part of the body works for every other part. How do you see that? In your mind. Knowledge goes beyond the senses. I will teach you to see with your mind's eye. Then you'll have no trouble seeing invisible things."

WHAT I LEARNED

To be spiritual you have to believe in something invisible. Baba taught me this at the very beginning. First you have to stop trusting that only your five senses are right. It's a hard habit to break, because common sense says, "I want to see it, touch it, taste it—then I'll know it's real." But I can make you taste something right now that is totally invisible.

Close your eyes and see a bright yellow lemon in your mind's eye. Now see a knife cutting the lemon into slices, and then see yourself biting into one slice. Did you notice that your mouth started watering? This happened exactly as if you were biting into an actual lemon. All it took was a mental picture, which you produced out of nowhere, and suddenly your body went into action. Millions of cells in your brain formed the image; a signal was sent along the network of nerves inside your head to your mouth; your salivary glands received the message and began to flow.

Here are some amazing facts that follow from this simple experiment:

There was no picture of a lemon inside your head. When you thought of a lemon, your brain cells didn't paint an image or project one on a screen. Your brain is as dark as the blackest cave—there's no light or color inside it. So where did that picture come from?

There was no taste of lemon in your mouth. You didn't actually experience real lemon juice. Your salivary glands, which you may think need food to react to, here needed nothing at all. So where did the sourness come from?

Someplace mysterious. Some place Baba was leading me to, step by step.

Everything Is Connected

Now, let's say you believe there really is *something* in the universe that you can't see," said Baba. "What does it do? If it had nothing to do, even if you called it God, our lives would stay the same as they are. People probably wouldn't bother looking for it in the first place."

"Probably not," I said.

The sun was rising higher in the sky, and we were comfortable sitting in the cool shade of the tree. Every once in a while I felt a darting worry about missing school, but as long as I kept listening to Baba, even this worry was far away.

"So it's a fine puzzle to figure out what this invisible *something* could be doing." Baba took in a big breath of air. "Go ahead, do that," he said. "The answer is right here, waiting to be noticed."

I took a deep breath. "I don't notice anything," I said.

"Isn't there something in the air?" asked Baba. "Spring.

You can't miss it. When the birds start singing and the buds come out on the trees, when hearts flutter and you see lovers holding hands in the park, isn't spring in the air?"

"Sure, but—"

"Well, why is it spring? There's no reason for it. The earth tilts a few degrees on its axis—so what? Yet in the arctic snow a polar bear knows that it is time to come out of hibernation. Flowers know that it is time to sprout without fear of dying in the frost. Locusts buried seven years in the ground know that it is time to creep forth. How can all this happen from a little tilt?"

Before I could hazard a guess, he said, "I'm going to show you. Imagine that you are a bird. You don't think about spring; you don't think in words at all. How do you know that it's time to fly north again and mate?"

"Spring fever?"

"Good enough," said Baba. "Let's call it an impulse that happens only in the spring. One impulse seems to strike every creature. The locust, the polar bear, the flower, and the bird live far apart, but they feel the same impulse in their own way. Even in the darkest depths of the ocean, where sunlight never reaches, the horseshoe crab knows that it's time to march hundreds of miles to shore, and on one single moonlit night millions of horseshoe crabs appear at once. Amazing.

"Sending that impulse is what *something* is doing. It

holds life together. That's its job. But now we can stop calling it *something*," said Baba. "Once you know what the invisible force does, you can call it by its rightful name."

"Which is what?" I asked.

"The soul."

WHAT I LEARNED

People have millions of things to say about the soul, but Baba focused on just one: The soul is the glue of the universe. It's not just sticky glue; it's intelligent. The universe is held together in three invisible ways:

Everything is connected.
Everything looks out for everything else.
Everything is in harmony with the whole.

Your body is a living example of how these three things work. A single cell that isn't connected, that selfishly looks out only for itself, and that refuses to be in harmony with the whole turns into a cancer. One rogue cell among billions is enough to destroy the entire scheme of life. The body's intelligence breaks down, and that is far more devastating than physical harm. Fortunately, such runaway cells are very uncommon, less than one in a million, and the huge majority of these rogues do not survive. The body's inner intelligence knows exactly how life should be regulated for maximum survival.

Baba didn't say that the invisible glue must be called the soul. Other terms have come down through the ages: spirit, God, the divine spark, the breath of life. Often I use the word *essence*. When you reduce anything to its purest form, you have its essence. An armful of roses can be reduced to half an ounce of pure rose essence. There are billions of people living totally different lives. Yet soul or spirit is the purest part of being alive, no matter who you are. It's your essence.

It's strange that this essence is so hard to find. When we go around looking for it, we're like fish looking everywhere for water but never seeming to find it. I imagine the first fish to discover water happened to jump out of the ocean. Maybe a shark was chasing it, and the fish got desperate. When it splashed back into the sea, the fish had a thrilling moment of *Aha! So that's where the water is. I've been swimming in it all my life and never knew.*

That's what Baba did for me. Like a fish splashing back into the sea, I discovered that I'd been living with spirit, inside and out, all my life. It's everywhere, making sure that everything is connected. The light from a star billions of light-years away is the same light that makes plants grow here on Earth. The plants give food; the food allowed you to develop in your mother's womb; and today you look at those stars with the eyes that the stars gave you. There's the cosmic connection.

Did you know that with every breath you breathe, you

take in millions of atoms breathed out yesterday by someone in China? Those atoms were in another body, circulating in the blood or building a cell or perhaps making a baby. Without knowing it, you are connected to a baby who hasn't even been born yet. The water in your body has the same salt and mineral content as the ocean, which means you are carrying the ocean around inside you. The skin cells that you rubbed off with a towel this morning when you stepped out of the shower contain molecules that were once in the body of Jesus and Buddha and every other holy figure from the past.

So rejoice in the cosmic connection. See yourself on a beautiful spring day. You are full of new life and energy. The day feels perfect. Inside you a spark is gleaming, and you suddenly know for sure that you are alive in a world that is your home. At that moment you are truly tuned in. Baba taught me never to forget that feeling of being connected to everything.

And he was just getting started.

Soul Training

"Let's move!" Baba said, jumping to his feet. The old man had been sitting so still in his cross-legged pose that he seemed to be planted in the earth like the twisted tree itself. Now I had to run to catch up with him.

"You're going into training," he called over his shoulder.

"What kind of training?" I asked. He was taking me to a green meadow that fringed the woods.

"The best kind," he said. "Soul training. Not many can teach it, so you must be very, very lucky. Did you know you were that lucky?"

"Not really." I wasn't sure if he was teasing me.

Baba found a spot in the middle of the meadow and looked around. "This is good," he said. "Lie down right there."

I got flat on my back in the tall grass, wondering what would come next.

"Now gaze at the sky," said Baba. "Do you see the sun?"

"Sure." With the morning mist burned away, the sun was right above me.

Baba took his hands and placed them over my eyes. "Now can you see the sun?" he asked.

"No, of course not."

"Session over," he said, looking pleased, as if I had done something extremely promising.

I protested. "What kind of training was that? Nothing happened."

Baba was always happiest when he had me a little off balance—I was learning that quick enough. He said, "When you cover your eyes, you can't see the sun, but you still know it's there. Nothing has happened to it, right?"

"So far," I said.

"If the sun went behind a cloud for weeks or months, you'd still know that you were connected to it," he said. I agreed. "The same is true for the soul. Just because you hide it doesn't mean it stops existing. Be prepared," he said. "Let's see if we can move some clouds."

Baba reached down and made the same motion of putting his hands over my eyes, only this time he put them over my heart.

Hold on, I thought.

With a bold flourish he took his hands away. Before I could think anything, I felt a coolness blow over me. I looked around. The meadow was rippling with soft waves of light. They seemed to be everywhere, and yet they were so faint it could have been a mirage.

"How did you do that?" I whispered. It was like somebody was shining a light from behind all the familiar things—grass, trees, sky—that I knew so well. A gray veil was gone, and yet I never knew it existed.

"I didn't do anything," Baba said. I felt his finger tap lightly near my heart. "The only beauty in the world is the beauty inside you. You can cloud over your soul; then the beauty disappears. But like the sun, it never goes away."

I tried to look inside the place he had touched. For a second I did see something. A small, flickering flame near my heart. The next instant it was gone. I sat up, and the meadow was just a meadow again.

"Was that real?" I asked shakily.

"You just got the faintest glimpse of what is real," said Baba. "The soul's light is as ever-present as the sun. Once you finish your training, you'll see what I mean, and much more. There is really only one soul, which each person has a piece of, and yet it is enough to light up the world."

What I Learned

That was the first time Baba let me catch a glimpse of my soul. From then on I wanted to see it as clearly as he did. Even though I never again experienced a green meadow rippling with waves of light, I kept a memory of how sweet that moment was. The soul doesn't wink in and out. It is our essence, the purest part of us. All the beautiful things in this world merely reflect it.

I have come to know other ways to catch a glimpse of the soul. Whenever the world around me tingles with life, I am really seeing a bit of my soul. When a stranger catches my eye and I see a glimmer of joy, I am really seeing a bit of my soul. When the light sparkles off the ocean like jewels or the air brushes over my skin like a caress, I am seeing a bit of my soul.

More than 90 percent of people believe they have a soul, according to opinion polls. So why do so many feel anxious, depressed, and generally out of tune? Countless answers have been given, but the spiritual answer is that the soul connection has been lost. By "lost" I mean "misplaced," since you can't really lose your soul. When it comes down to it, Baba taught me that there are three ways I could choose to live:

I could put my hands over my eyes and never see my soul. This would be like a permanently cloudy day, when you never see the sun.

I could see my soul by glimpses. This would be like lying under a tree and seeing the sun dart in and out between the leaves.

I could see my soul all the time. This is like looking at the sun with nothing to block your view.

Which way of life I chose would make a huge difference. When the soul isn't in sight, people have to struggle to find meaning. They feel anxious and lost. They wonder if there really is anything worth believing in. When the soul darts in and out of view, life improves. People feel less depressed, more in tune with everything. But the situation remains shaky because dark times will come, and then life seems unsafe and unfair. I came to Baba knowing that terrible things happen in the world. On the happiest day of spring you can turn on the news and find scenes of terrible warfare. So I naturally thought I had a good idea of how things were.

Today I can still turn on the TV and find scenes of terrible warfare. But Baba took my hands away from my soul, and I see something else, too. Something that no amount of darkness can blot out. *Spirit never goes away.* Clouds may hide it from sight, but they can't destroy it. They can't even alter it by one little bit. That's the third, and best, way to be—secure in your soul. If you still have doubts, follow me on the next step of Baba's soul training.

The Way of the Heart

"The best way to live is the way your soul wants you
to," Baba said.

We were still in the meadow, me lying lazily in the tall
sweetgrass, Baba sitting cross-legged on a large rock
watching me. "I don't divide people into those who believe
and those who don't," he said. "I divide them into those
who know how to live and those who don't."

I sat up and faced him. "So if I asked my soul what I
should do today, it would tell me?"

"Maybe," Baba said. "But your soul isn't an answer box. It
wants you to walk your own path and still have the best life.
There are four ways of doing that. The first is known as the way
of the heart. If you listen, your ears will tell you how it works."

My ears? But Baba didn't want any more questions. He
put his finger to his lips. I lay back down. I almost fell
asleep in the sweetness of the meadow, but then I heard two
voices in the distance. They were having a loud argument.

"Thief! You stole my money," the first one shouted.

"Idiot! I charged you a fair price," the second voice yelled back. "Leave me alone!"

I raised my head just enough to see who it was. Two men from the village were arguing in the road. Their faces were red, and they were close to fighting.

"Why are we listening to them?" I said in a low whisper. But Baba just put his fingers to his lips again, so I waited.

Still shouting, the two men went by without seeing us. Just then I heard more voices. They sounded like kids from my school going home for lunch (which was much more common in India back then).

"I still don't get it. They're just chatting and talking about stuff," I said, ducking my head so that no one could see me. Baba nodded without a word.

When the kids were gone, I waited some more, but there was nothing else to hear.

"On the contrary," said Baba, who was reading my mind so often that it was becoming normal. "Now is the time you must really listen."

He pointed toward the road. Again I raised my head, and this time I saw two young lovers from the village who had just become engaged. They were walking hand in hand, gazing at each other silently.

After they were past, Baba said, "People shout when their hearts are far apart. They speak normally when their hearts are in tune. But when two hearts are one, there is no need for words at all. That is how the way of the heart works. In silence you will find your soul as the love guiding you from your heart."

WHAT I LEARNED

The way of the heart isn't about words—it's about feelings. Your heart is the natural home of spirit. If you say to someone, "Show me where your soul is," almost without hesitation they will point to the heart. What they might not know is what the heart can really accomplish. Have you heard of horse whispering? When a wild horse is caught, someone has to break it in. Wild horses are afraid of the saddle; they panic and fight when they feel a rider on their back for the first time. So traditionally the sight of a horse being broken in was wild and violent.

Then someone discovered another way, called horse whispering. Instead of forcing the horse to obey, the trainer handles it gently, looking it in the eye, stroking its flanks to calm it down, and mounting the horse only when the trainer feels a signal from the animal that says, *You may get on me. I trust you.* The old, violent way of breaking horses took days; horse whispering can often get a wild horse to accept a saddle in a few hours.

What's at work here is the way of the heart, and the steps are the same with people as with horses:

Tune in to the other person.
Gain the other person's trust.
Be in harmony; do not resist the other person's feelings.

These three steps don't use words; in fact, words just get in the way. You have to be willing to enter someone else's world. That can sound scary, yet as you get used to the way of the heart you will see how naturally it works.

1. TUNE IN

The first step comes down to really looking and listening. The simple question "How do you feel?" is always a good start. But look and listen from the heart; that's the key. Someone may say, "I'm fine," yet if they look stiff, with arms folded and a tense tone in their voice, don't those things tell you more than words? If you look into someone's eyes—not staring, but just making contact—you begin to feel what they are feeling. Likewise, you have to listen from the heart, which tunes in to feelings all the time.

Whenever you meet anyone, your heart reaches out and asks: *Is this person feeling good or bad, excited or depressed, worried or expectant?* Everyone else's heart is doing the same thing. So don't get in the way or pretend that you don't notice. We all notice feelings at the heart level. Words are easily forgotten, but a look from the heart becomes part of who you are.

2. GAIN TRUST

When you open yourself to someone, trust begins to develop. Have you ever watched squirrels in the park? If you throw a peanut at one, it will scamper away and keep its distance, wondering if you are to be trusted. But if you hold the peanut in your open hand, the squirrel will dart closer, then run away, then come closer again. After a moment even a skittish squirrel will be eating out of your hand.

With people it takes an open heart instead of a peanut, but you hold it out just as patiently and just as still. We're all afraid at times to show our feelings when we think they will make us look weak or set us up for rejection. But if you simply allow yourself to be with someone else, quietly and with an open heart, trust comes naturally.

Think about someone in your life who leaves an open space for you to be yourself. No one is more valuable. I would much rather have a pillar of trust in my life than a pillar of strength. So test the waters and find someone who will, first, listen to you and, second, accept what you're feeling.

3. BE IN HARMONY

The third step comes down to acceptance. In the joining of two hearts there is always acceptance. This is because neither one is thinking, *I can't waste my valuable time putting up with you.* When you are in harmony, you have as much time for another person as for yourself. Lovers don't need to speak because they feel like one person. What if you aren't in love? You can still close the gap between yourself and anyone you meet. *Feel what the other person feels.* If you do this without judging, then the same thing always happens. You realize, *I've felt that way too.* Now you are in harmony.

It's human nature to sit in judgment, but it's also human nature to rise above judgment. The choice is yours. Judging means making somebody else inferior. If you can't stand it because somebody around you is crying or depressed or criticizing all the time, stop and ask yourself, "Am I better than that?" If you say yes, you are judging them. And they know it, because in their heart they read your secret feeling of superiority.

Yet the truth is that all of us have cried, thrown an angry fit, and criticized others. Feelings happen. When you accept them as a part of life, you can begin to accept other people, and in time *all* people, from the heart. I sometimes think the world could be changed overnight if the Golden Rule said, "Feel about others as you would have them feel about you." Certainly this is what my heart is thinking, and yours, too, if I am not mistaken.

The Way of the Mind

"**Y**our soul is always sending you messages," Baba remarked. "Some everyday thoughts are actually these soul messages. Did you know that? They are the second way your soul wants you to live by, the way of the mind."

I had gotten very hungry, and yet before I told him, Baba produced a large handkerchief from his pocket. When he opened it, I was surprised to see some flatbread wrapped around curried potatoes, with even a bit of mango pickle packed inside to give it tang—not too sour, not too bitter. He broke the bread in half, and we began eating contentedly.

"What kind of messages?" I asked.

"You never can tell," said Baba. "The soul likes to be unpredictable. It likes to keep you excited about turning the next page of your life. So you have to keep an open mind. That's the key to the second way."

"I have an open mind, but I don't get any messages," I protested.

"Ah." Suddenly Baba clapped his two hands together, and when they came apart, the right one held a bright gold coin. "Would you like to have this?"

"Sure," I said quickly, wondering why he had changed the subject.

"I'll give it to you if you can count backward by threes from a hundred," he said.

"That's all?" I asked suspiciously. The coin looked large and valuable; it reminded me of pirate's gold.

"All? If you can do this, you will prove that you have mastered the way of the mind." Baba raised his forefinger in the air like a starter's pistol at a race. "Starting now."

There was no time for hesitation. "All right," I said. "One hundred, ninety-seven, ninety-four, ninety-one . . ." Baba let me go on for a while, just watching. But when I got to seventy-six, he leaned toward me and began to whisper in my ear.

He was whispering numbers at random: "Twenty-seven, five, forty-eight . . ." I tried to pay attention to what I was doing, but it was hopeless, and I lost count.

"Too bad," he said. "You got distracted." He slipped the gold coin into his pocket.

"Let me try again," I entreated. "I'll really concentrate this time." Baba nodded, and I started counting backward, only this time I put my hands over my ears and closed my eyes to shut out any distractions.

"One hundred, ninety-seven, ninety-four—ow! What are you doing?"

I hadn't gotten more than three numbers when Baba reached his hand toward my head as if he were going to pluck out a hair. I stumbled and lost count.

"Sorry," he said. "I guess I made you nervous."

"How do you expect me to get this right when I have to worry about you snatching my hair?" I said.

Baba rose to his feet. "I'll stand over there so you won't have any distractions or worries. Good enough?"

"All right," I said warily, thinking he probably had another trick up his sleeve.

"No more tricks," said Baba, reading my mind. He walked three paces away. "Just begin where you left off."

"I don't remember where I left off," I said.

He looked pleased. "Now you know why people don't receive the messages being sent by the soul. They are too distracted or too worried or too forgetful. Only when you become free of those obstacles will you have an open mind. Then you will be master of the second way."

He took the coin from his pocket and flipped it toward me in a slow, high arc, and to my credit I caught it on the first try, despite all the trouble Baba had put me through.

What I Learned

This lesson surprised me because I assumed that the way of the mind was about thinking. But Baba told me he himself didn't have a head full of thoughts, not even wise thoughts. His mind was open, which means awake, alert, ready for anything. *That,* he told me, is the only way to tune in to the soul's messages.

The way of the mind gave me three things to do, or rather to *stop* doing. I should stop being distracted. I should stop worrying. I should stop forgetting. These three things block the mind by putting people in a kind of fog. Later on I could practically see this fog, for everyone has friends who wander around distracted all the time, those who worry all the time, and those who never seem to remember anything, especially when it's important. If you lose track of your soul, Baba said, how can you expect it to help you?

1. BEING DISTRACTED

Distractions are everywhere, and it's easy to get caught up in them. You'll hear that kids today are addicted to computer games the way an earlier generation was addicted to talking on the phone. But either way, the reason for any distraction is usually the same: The mind finds it hard to focus.

Talking to your friend is more pleasant than mowing the grass. Almost anything on the computer is more fun than homework. A distraction is basically a sidetrack or detour, and kids usually take them on purpose (adults do too!). Billions of dollars are spent every year to provide us with movies, TV shows, games, and amusement parks— we are willing to pay a lot to be distracted.

As much fun as these things are, you might ask yourself, "Do I really want to be detoured from who I am?" The soul is part of you. It wants to give you everything. Should you pay to lose touch with it? This is a choice every kid must think about. When you're totally focused on a computer game, what happens if your dad wants to talk to you? You probably can't pull yourself away very easily, and when you do, you feel put upon and annoyed.

Now consider this: Your soul speaks a lot softer than your parents, and it never pounds on the door, as frustrated parents will do if they can't get your attention. A little distraction is all it takes to lose track of the soul. Baba taught me that a moment of real attention, when you truly listen to what's inside you, is worth an hour of wandering down the long detour road of distraction.

2. WORRYING

Every kid knows the dreaded words "Wait until your father gets home." They weren't said too often in my house growing up, but it takes only a few times to understand how worry works. You're on pins and needles. Nothing bad has happened to you yet, but you're sure it's going to.

Your soul doesn't want you to worry. Worry is unreal. It makes you feel pain in advance, and your soul isn't part of anything painful. Survivors who have been through a disaster like a flood or tornado will tell you that handling the crisis was ten times easier than waiting for it to occur.

So the best way to cure worry is to confront the thing you fear.

Worry goes away when you face the thing you fear. Once you know how you're going to deal with a situation, your soul will help bring you a sense of security; it will help make you feel safe. See yourself in the situation. Practice what you're going to do and say. Be totally honest about what you know is true. Every time your mind says, *What if?* answer it with, "Then, I'll do X."

The more concrete you are with facing your fear, the better. Some champion athletes visualize a whole game in advance before stepping out on the field. Singers practice their songs, actors recite their lines. Of course, a part of you will say, "Just don't think about it." But have you really succeeded in not thinking about something you dread? Your mind keeps coming back to it no matter how hard you try.

Above all, know that you'll survive, no matter what. And if you doubt that, seek someone you trust so that you can hear them say it to you. Their reassurance is an echo of what your soul is telling you.

3. Forgetting

Forgetting your soul is hard to describe. It's like being a millionaire who thinks he's poor because he doesn't remember what's in the bank. It's like looking for your glasses and forgetting that you are already wearing them.

In other words, it's a special kind of forgetting. When you forget that you left your wallet at the supermarket, it might still be there when you go back, or it might not. You feel anxious not knowing which it's going to be. But your soul is always there, ready for you to remember it. The way of the mind could be called the way of reminding— you remind yourself that your spirit is always present; it is in, around, and everywhere. The whole universe vibrates with every thought, according to physics. The messages sent by your soul are sometimes sudden flashes, sometimes just a steady feeling that tells you, deep in your heart, that you belong, you are safe, you are part of everything. All it takes to receive these messages is never to forget that your soul is sending them.

The Way of Silence

We were back in the shade under the trees because it was the hottest part of the day. Baba had stopped talking. He sat very, very still now. I watched as a single leaf fell from the tree. It fluttered and swiveled through the air as it dropped. Baba saw it too.

"Do you think you can catch that?" he asked.

I knew how hard it is to catch a falling leaf, because I had tried before. I grabbed at it, but the next puff of air seemed to carry the leaf just out of reach—nothing is more slippery than a leaf that doesn't want to be caught.

"Can you?" I asked when my try was over.

A second leaf was falling toward us. Baba didn't reach up or even look at it. When the leaf was just in front of his face, his hand darted out, and as easy as that, he caught it.

"You see?" he said. "I am just like a snake in the sun. One moment I am so still that I could be sleeping, but when I strike, I move instantly, with total certainty. Now you know the key to the third way that your soul wants you to live by, the way of silence."

"I don't think being quiet makes somebody certain," I said doubtfully.

"You haven't found the real silence yet," he said. "It's a lot more than being quiet. Silence sharpens the mind like an arrow ready to fly through the air. But it also softens the mind, like the paw of a cat when its claws are drawn in. A cat's paw is sensitive and sharp at the same time."

"But nobody is really certain of anything, are they?" I asked.

"No?" said Baba. "Haven't you set eyes on somebody and instantly said to yourself, 'He's going to be my new best friend'? Haven't you woken up one morning and known for sure that something special was going to happen to you? The soul has a quality. *It knows for sure.*

"The way of silence is about developing the ability to know for sure," said Baba. "You can learn to be relaxed and still, yet when it's time to make a decision, you will be able to *go!* Just like that."

WHAT I LEARNED
The way of silence isn't about being quiet for its own sake. Silence is how you are naturally when you are certain about something, because the mind keeps talking only as long as it is in doubt. Baba was really teaching me about being a spiritual warrior. That's a term you may have read

or heard about. Spiritual warriors aren't fighting other people; they're fighting not to be mentally foggy and doubtful. So it's not a martial art.

Instead, spiritual warriors are training to know who they are. When you're certain about that one thing, the rest is simple. In India there's an ancient saying, "I am That." What it means is that if you strip away all labels, you are pure spirit or essence. People usually say, "I *have* a soul," but the spiritual warrior says, "I *am* the soul." This wisdom is one of the most glorious goals you can live for. In ancient India they would have said, "Yes, it's true. I am That" to mean the same thing.

You've seen pictures, I'm sure, of Buddhist monks in saffron robes meditating or of Christian monks in silent prayer. Both are connecting with That. They are in training to awaken all the qualities of spirit. And That is intelligent beyond anything we can imagine. It breathes life into raw matter. The sugar in a sugar bowl is basically the same as the sugar that your brain uses for food (in the body this sugar is called glucose), and yet there has been a magical change in it. The sugar in the sugar bowl just sits there. The sugar in your brain turns into music, painting, science, architecture—all the greatest accomplishments of human beings. And it turns into love, which is more mysterious than any of these.

Being certain isn't something you can force. You can decide to act confident all the time, but that's not the same thing. You hold the power to transform That into anything you want. The tools are simple: You think, you feel, you act. Everyone uses these very tools every moment. But to master how they work—that's the skill of a spiritual warrior. Like any other skill, it must be learned and practiced. The way of silence asks you to dedicate yourself to learning what That can do.

Perhaps you thought prayer was just a way to ask God for something or that meditation was just a way to become peaceful inside. Their scope is much, much larger. Prayer and meditation are ways of saying, "Turn me into something special. I want to be transformed." You say this to God, to your soul, and to yourself at the same time. Since all three are made of That, all three are listening to your request, and so you start to be transformed from that moment on.

You don't have to be silent all the time, but if you want to watch yourself turning into something special, it's good to be silent for a few minutes every day. I like to sit quietly on my own and easily follow my breath as it goes in and out. I do this for ten minutes usually, sitting with my eyes closed and gently feeling the cool flow of my breath. I don't fight against thoughts if they come to me; if I feel a sensation anywhere in my body, I let my attention go there without fighting that, either. It's a simple thing, yet day by day the silence has gotten deeper. It will deepen for you, too, and you will begin to gain a certainty that is very precious, the certainty that what is special about you is That, the very soul in everything.

The Way of Action

"The fourth way that your soul wants you to live by is the way of action," said Baba. "Everyone must act, yet not all actions are spiritual."

"What's the difference?" I asked.

Without answering, Baba pointed upward. I looked, and overhead a small brown bird was watching us from a branch. Baba had stopped talking; his attention was completely captured by the bird. So I thought I'd better watch too.

The bird was a kind of sparrow. After a few seconds it got bored with us and began darting back and forth. Soon I saw why. It was carrying tiny bits of grass and twigs to build a nest. There was no rhyme or reason to this project though. The bird rushed here and there in aimless zigzags. Sometimes it stopped to eat a seed it had chanced upon. The next minute it spotted another sparrow and flew at it to drive it away, providing fifteen seconds of excitement. Before long the bird remembered that it was supposed to be nest-building, and back it would go for another tuft of dry grass.

"What do you think?" Baba asked after a while.

"That bird is all over the place," I said.

"Yes, it never pays attention to any kind of plan, does it?" Baba said. "It flies wherever the next impulse takes it. I see a miracle in that."

"Why? All I see is a flighty bird," I said.

Baba shook his head. "When you can follow your next impulse and still have heaven watch over you, that's the very best miracle. It's the way of action carried out perfectly. That bird has no plan in life and no worries. It follows its instincts, and somehow everything gets done very well."

I had a hard time thinking that way. "Then, why do people have to make plans and worry?" I asked.

"The problem isn't with plans," said Baba. "It's with forgetting that life is meant to be carefree. What you want right now should also be the best thing that could happen to you. Then you'd be living the same miracle as a bird or any other creature. Better, in fact, because creatures can't choose to change, and you can."

"How do I do that, Baba?" I asked.

But he only kept gazing at the sparrow, which barely stopped its zigzagging for a second. "We've been here a long time," Baba said. "Your day is up, and I promised to keep you only one day. Now you know the four ways of the soul. Go home and think about them."

"Wait," I said. "What if we had a second day? What would you teach me then?"

"How to get what you want," said Baba. "The four ways of the soul have a practical side. You might be interested in that."

I was, of course. "How will I find you? Will you be here tomorrow?" I asked.

But Baba had jumped to his feet. The sparrow decided to fly off into the deep woods, and the old man had nothing else on his mind except to follow it. He took one last look at me over his shoulder, and a moment later both of them disappeared into the shadowy gloom of the forest.

WHAT I LEARNED

The last thing you might expect from the way of action is that it's about miracles. It's a very beautiful idea to think that miracles can happen. But at some point you have to decide if miracles are going to happen to *you*. Baba thought they could. To him, every day is a miracle if you have the soul on your side. Then your actions change because they start coming from your soul.

In practical terms this is what action from the soul feels like:

1. You act impeccably. This means that you do your best, never cheating, never cutting corners, never

letting someone else take responsibility for what is yours.

2. You give your action to others. In place of selfishness you offer what you do in service. You show devotion to those who love you. You accomplish things on behalf of your vision.

3. You find your unique talent and remain true to it.

4. You don't worry about reward or praise. Someone once said, very truly, that if you want to be a success, make someone else a success.

5. You focus on the journey rather than the destination. This means that you keep your attention on the very thing you are doing now, getting everything out of this moment, rather than focusing on events and things that haven't happened yet.

6. You always have the inner attitude that your actions come from the universe and go back to the universe.

7. You don't hold on, you don't clutch and cling to anything. Your purpose is to be the caretaker of everything valuable in your life, cherishing it but knowing that in the end no one possesses anything. The only thing you can truly possess is yourself.

A sparrow, or any creature, doesn't work at getting things to go right. The next impulse that comes its way is exactly what creatures should do. When you can match that, you have mastered the way of action. There is more complication in your life than in a sparrow's, but the same infinite intelligence is capable of making even the most complex life beautiful, peaceful, well ordered, and fulfilled. You don't have to fight and struggle for everything. You can trust that you will always find a way. You can be at peace that whatever comes to you is right. You can feel that your inner yearnings are understood and will unfold in time as they should.

So really, Baba gave me a whole vision in the example of one tiny sparrow. If I could find a way to be carefree and still accomplish what I wanted to do, my whole life would feel like a miracle. After our first day together, I could only imagine what he had in mind for our second.

Day Two

How Do Wishes Come True?

Life Is Desire

Baba didn't make me wait long. It was only a few days later that he returned. Only, this time I didn't find him under the twisted tree by the side of the road. He came to me.

I was back at school. Nobody had called me in for missing a day; how this magic occurred I will never know. Maybe Baba knew a lot more tricks than I imagined. When the noon bell rang, I burst outside with the other boys—we had no girls at our school on the hill—tearing off my tie as I ran toward the soccer field.

I was in the backfield waiting for the kickoff when something caught my eye. A speck of white in the distance. Baba was watching us from the flat roof of the school. Everyone else was so caught up in the game that they didn't notice. Or maybe Baba was just for my eyes. Either way, I ran off the field and ignored the shouts that followed me from the rest of my team.

When I opened the creaky door that led on to the roof,

I half expected Baba not to be there. But he was, sitting calmly on the parapet.

"Some come true, but many never do," he said. He had barely turned his head to acknowledge my arrival. "Do you know what I'm talking about?"

"No." I was now used to Baba's habit of mystifying me.

"Wishes," he said. "Look down there."

He pointed at the soccer game, which was a mad, screaming scramble. Boys ran up and down the field and kicked the ball as if everything was at stake. "It doesn't matter what's at stake," Baba said, picking up my thought. "When you really want something, it's hard to get your mind off it. Every moment counts until your wish comes true."

"But many never do," I said, repeating his words. "Isn't that how life works?"

"No," said Baba. "When your wish doesn't come true, you've gone against the way life works. Let me show you."

His finger had found a tuft of grass growing between two bricks in the parapet. "A seed landed up here, where there's no soil. It sprouted in a pinch of dust between these bricks. A little rain found this cranny, and now there is an explosion of life." He flicked at the grass with his finger. "Each blade is so fragile that you can crush it with a tiny squeeze, yet this grass has all of life behind it. The power of life is irresistible. Go to the city and you'll see wisps of grass pushing their way between tons of concrete in the roads that cars roll over every day."

"But that's what grass does," I said. "What does it have to do with a wish?"

"Life has one overwhelming desire," said Baba, "which is to grow. Your wishes are part of life, and they deserve to have its power behind them."

"So you're saying every wish should come true?"

"I am," said Baba.

"But they can't." I pointed down at the soccer field. "Both sides want to win. They fight to make that wish come true. Yet in the end one side has to lose. For them the wish doesn't come true."

"That's very true," said Baba. "But you've left out the *X* factor, the unknown. The *X* factor is spiritual. It turns failures into victories, because in the deeper reality all wishes *must* come true. They have no choice."

"That's quite a mystery," I said.

"One worth exploring on our second day, if you feel ready," said Baba.

He didn't wait for an answer. Five minutes later he'd led me off the roof and down the stairs. We strode quickly away from the school, and the shouts from the soccer field faded into faint echoes.

WHAT I LEARNED

Baba had a lot to say about how wishes come true. This encounter wasn't really a lesson, but it taught me something important even before we had begun. I stopped seeing life around me as routine and mechanical. Does anyone really bother about a bit of grass growing through the sidewalk? It's just there. But every seed of grass is bursting with desire. It *must* expand and grow. It seizes any chance to sprout. It uses any opportunity to get around obstacles. Desires are seeds just like that—they want to make something happen, and even when the desire is small and insignificant, it doesn't want to stop until it gets to its goal.

So the wonder is not that all of us have so many wishes, hopes, and dreams. The wonder is that they don't come true all the time. Baba believed that they should. No, they *must,* because the irresistible power of life is never going to take no for an answer. If you have taken no for an answer—and all of us have—then spirit wants to change how you see yourself. Only one side can win a soccer game, but there's a catch: The *X* factor is at work, and what you see on the surface isn't always what you get.

The Wishing Tree

We were walking down the road toward the village when Baba asked, "What would you wish for if you could wish for anything? Would you wish for riches?"

"Yes," I said without a moment's hesitation.

"Would you wish to be popular and famous?"

"Yes, that sounds pretty good too," I said.

He smiled. "In fairy tales there are always three wishes. What would your third one be?"

"Promise you won't tell anybody, but I'd wish for someone to love me," I said.

"Deeply?" asked Baba. "You must be precise." I felt my cheeks get warm. Before I could stammer out anything, Baba said, "Very well, deeply it is. Three wishes to work on. Now, let me see."

He began to scan the horizon like an old sea captain searching for port. "It's around here somewhere. Ah," he said, pointing to the tallest tree in the distance. "We need him."

We left the road and tramped across a field until we

55

reached the tree. Baba said, "This is a wishing tree. It's been giving people what they want for a long, long time."

"Are you sure you didn't just make that up?" I was getting used to Baba's mischievous tactics.

Baba pointed to the bark, which had deep slashes hacked into it. "That's how I know this is a wishing tree," he said, launching into the following explanation:

Wishing trees go back many centuries in India, although for modern people they are now more legend than fact. Everyone in this part of the country had been told about wishing trees by their grandmothers, and perhaps belief was stronger here. For one day a villager was walking alone, dreaming about his future. He stopped to rest under a tree and thought, "If only I were rich."

When he returned home, to his amazement he found a mansion where his hut had stood, and inside the mansion was every kind of treasure. Immediately he knew that he had found the wishing tree. The young man told no one where his wealth had come from. He left the village that night, never to be seen there again.

"But a year later," Baba said, "he returned with an ax and began to hack at the tree, cursing it all the while. 'You never told me that people would envy my money, and now I am miserable,' he cried. 'I trust no one, I cannot tell if anyone likes me for myself or only for my riches. Night and day I worry that I might lose everything, because I know nothing of how to handle money.'"

He chopped at the tree until he was exhausted. But the tree would not fall.

Time passed, and one day a young woman from the village was wandering in the woods. She sat under the tree to rest, and a wish came to her. "If only I were famous. It would be so wonderful to be the most popular woman in the world."

When she got home, her house was swarmed with TV cameras and reporters. A huge crowd was gathering, and as soon as they spied the young woman, she was mobbed by screaming fans. Breathlessly she made it into her house. The next day she emerged to find that the cameras and reporters were still there. She waved and got into a limousine and was never seen in the village again.

"But a year later," said Baba, "she sneaked back to the wishing tree with an ax in her hand. She began to chop at it, cursing all the while. 'You didn't tell me that nobody would ever leave me alone. I can't go anywhere without being stared at, my slightest misfortune is blown up into a tragedy in the newspapers, and hundreds of people a day ask for my help, when I can barely manage my own life. I'm so miserable.'"

She chopped at the tree until she was exhausted. But the tree would not fall.

More time passed. Then it chanced that a young mother-to-be was wandering in the woods. She rested under the tree, dreaming of the joys of having a baby. *I want nothing in this world but the love of my baby and my husband,* she thought. *If only they will love me forever.*

She went home, and her husband greeted her with hugs and kisses. Two weeks later their baby was born, and the minute she opened her eyes, she gazed on her mother with adoration.

Much more time passed before the mother returned to the woods.

"It took five years," said Baba, "and then she came back in tattered rags, furiously hacking at the tree with an ax and cursing it. 'My husband loves me so much that he can't bear to leave my side to go to work. Now we have no money. My little child cries without end unless I am with her every waking moment. Although they love me truly, I have no peace. I am the most miserable woman on earth.'"

She, too, kept chopping until she was exhausted, but the tree didn't fall. Baba rubbed his hand over the wounds she had left behind.

"Do you know what went wrong?" he said. "They all wished for externals, and that's what the tree gave them. Each had an outer image of being rich, famous, and loved, but images are not what your soul wants for you. You must wish from the inside, then the highest wisdom will be at your command."

What I Learned

This lesson was about the difference between a wish that helps you and one that doesn't. All three people who found the wishing tree got what they wished for, and so their lives changed, but only on the outside. They forgot to wish for inner change. No matter how much money he had, the rich man wasn't rich inside. No matter how famous she was, the celebrity didn't feel worthy inside. No matter how much other people loved her, the mother didn't know how to love herself.

Baba taught me that my soul hears all my wishes from the inside. The soul hears what people *really* want, which means in their heart of hearts. After I grew up, I heard about an interesting study in this area. People were asked the question "What do you want?" Then no matter what answer they gave, they were asked why. So the questioning might go like this:

Q. *What do you think you want right now?*
A. *I want a great body.*

Q. *Why?*
A. *Because I'd be more attractive and confident.*

Q. *Why?*
A. *Because people would notice me, and that's important.*

Q. *Why?*
A. *Because it makes me happy, and I want to be happy.*

What the experimenters found is that if you ask the question "Why?" often enough, everybody winds up saying the same thing: "Because I want to be happy." It doesn't matter what they start out wanting—money, popularity, fame, a better job. In the end all wishes are for happiness.

Baba taught me that if what you really want is happiness, why not get it directly? The place where happiness is always available is inside yourself. You have to create your own joy. Possessions can't do it for you, and neither can other people. Naturally, you feel happy with your friends or when you buy something you coveted. But these periods of happiness are temporary. Your soul knows this, which is why it leads you to the root of happiness, not to its leaves and branches.

On the outside life will always be fickle, which is another reason not to plant your happiness there. I heard a story once: Four brothers came to a wise man and said, "Our grandfather died and left us a hundred pieces of gold. But he didn't say how the money should be divided. Can you tell us the best way?"

The wise man said, "Do you want it divided the way most people would do it or the way God would do it?"

"We want the way God would do it," said the four brothers.

So the wise man gave eighty pieces of gold to the first brother, fifteen to the second brother, four to the third brother, and only one piece of gold to the last brother.

"This is how God would do it?" they said in astonishment.

"Yes," said the wise man. "If you'd asked for the way most people would do it, I'd have given you all an equal share!"

The nice things of this world are not divided equally. Some people get more than their share, while others get less. But this pertains only to outward desires. On the inside everyone can win a life that brings equal joy and happiness. Baba told me to wish for just one thing: "Make me rich inside," which means as full of joy and satisfaction as possible. He told me that my soul would help me every day to make this wish come true, no matter how many outward things came my way or not.

Follow the Thread

"Even without a wishing tree there's a magical way to make a wish come true," said Baba. He held his hand out. "Here," he said. "I'll give it to you."

"I don't see anything," I said.

"I'm handing you a string; you can't see it because it's invisible," he said. He wasn't satisfied until I pretended to pick up the invisible string dangling from his palm and put it in mine.

"Now all you have to do is follow the string. It will lead to what you want."

I was bewildered. "What if I want a car? I'm too young to drive. There are almost no cars in the village and no dealership in a hundred miles. How will this string get me a car?"

"It will," Baba said with smiling confidence. "Let me show you how."

We had been walking down the road for a while, and I could almost see the outskirts of the village up ahead.

Baba started searching for something in the bushes. "Ah, here we go," he exclaimed.

I went over to where he was standing. "A spiderweb?" I said.

"That's right, and where is the spider?" asked Baba. The web was suspended between two bushes, and it looked freshly made that morning. "After finishing her web, the spider weaves one last thread. She follows it to a hiding place and sits, holding tight to her thread. She's waiting for it to vibrate, and when it does," said Baba, "she knows she's caught her prey."

If I looked very closely, I could just see the thread he was talking about, although I still couldn't spy its weaver.

"Now, what would happen if you cut that tiny, nearly invisible thread?" asked Baba. "She'd be cut off from all her hard work."

"That's true," I said, holding up my hand with the invisible string in it. "But this string doesn't lead anywhere."

"Oh, yes it does," said Baba. "Your soul has woven that string. It leads to what you want. Stay connected to your soul and you will find, step by step, that you are being led to your deepest desires. But if you cut the string, it leads nowhere."

WHAT I LEARNED
I knew what Baba meant about the spiderweb, but it took a long while to figure out how my invisible string worked.

Like getting a car. Baba knew that I would have to wait a few years, take driving lessons, pass my test, and then hope that my father would help me buy my own car. These steps followed one upon the other. Each step was necessary, and each unfolded in its own time. So following the thread was no problem.

Let's take it a bit further. What about wishes that are much harder to make come true? In my family there was an impossible dream that changed everybody's life, and I will tell you its story to illustrate how amazing a thread can be.

Many years ago there was a young man from India who wanted more than anything to be a doctor. He went to school and got his degree, but then a war came along, he went into the army, and there was no way for him to finish his studies.

As it happened, the young man was assigned as an aide to the most important official in the country, the British viceroy of India. When the war was over, the viceroy, who had ruled over millions of people, turned to his aide and said, "You've done me good service. Is there anything I can do for you? Just ask."

Without hesitation the young man spoke up. He wanted to be trained in advanced medicine alongside the British doctors, he said. The viceroy granted him his wish, but when he got to the training hospital, everyone ignored this quiet Indian who didn't even belong there. Day after day he studied hard. He knew the answers to every question, but he was never called on.

One day the medical students were trailing behind one of the most famous British doctors as he reviewed his cases. Senior doctors made rounds of the hospital wards every morning with students in tow like ducklings. They got to a certain patient, and the famous doctor said, "Who can tell me what's wrong with this man?"

It was a difficult case, and none of the British students volunteered. But the young Indian's hand was up, so he had to be called on, and he knew the right answer. After that his teachers paid attention to him. One day the famous British doctor called him into his office.

"I'm returning home to England tomorrow," the famous doctor told him, "and you've impressed me. Is there anything I can do for you? Just ask."

For the second time in his life the young man saw that his wish might come true. He asked to go to London to study how to become a heart specialist. Which is how my father, Krishan Chopra, found himself on a boat to England and a career as one of India's first heart doctors.

Did this chain of events happen by accident? Baba taught me not to think that way. My father was helped by his soul. If he remained true to his wish, which came from deep in his heart, there would be a way to make it come true.

Everyone has wishes and dreams, and making them come true is important. It's important to your soul as well.

But it doesn't offer its help in a loud voice—in fact, it doesn't give advice at all. Instead it sets out a path that you can follow, and thus you find, step by step, that your wish is beginning to unfold as reality.

When any dream has come true for me, I notice the following stages:

> *I asked inside for what I wanted.*
>
> *I was precise, and my wish really meant something to me.*
>
> *I let go of my wish so that the universe could compute how to make it come true. In other words, I got out of the way.*
>
> *I didn't waste time fantasizing about the future.*
>
> *I looked for even the smallest opening that showed the possibility of success. No opportunity was too small, and I didn't hold back because I was waiting for something bigger and better.*
>
> *I didn't wait for a payoff. If my desire changed before it came true, then I changed my expectations. Not every wish has to come true as I imagine it. I wait for the moment of fulfillment, which says, "Okay, that's all I really wanted."*
>
> *I looked for help everywhere, even in chance encounters, small coincidences, and sudden openings I never thought would come my way.*
>
> *I was grateful for every small step of accomplishment.*

All these steps may sound a bit complicated, but they're based on a simple theme: Your soul wants your wishes to come true, and it wants to make the journey as easy and natural as possible. It took many years for me to see that this whole pattern, from the planting of a seed to its final fruit, is all planned and handled by my soul. That's why Baba considered the invisible string to be one of the best-kept secrets of spirit.

Trust Your Soul

For most people the hardest part about wishing is to trust that it works," said Baba. "But right this moment you are asking for something and trusting that you will receive it. Every time you take a breath, for instance, you are asking for air. Does the air refuse?"

"No," I said.

"When you lift your arm, you are asking your muscles to move. Do your muscles refuse?"

"No."

"So wishes are being answered all the time with perfect trust," he said. "We live in a world of desires coming true."

As I looked around it was easy to believe what Baba was saying. We had stopped in the center of the village. Shops were everywhere, and people were spending money and bustling home with what they had bought.

"See how many wishes will come true today?" he said.

"But these people worked hard for their money," I said.

"They don't think that buying something means trusting it to come from God."

"They would get much more if they did," he said. "When you trust that your soul is helping you to make your wishes come true, half the work is done."

"I don't know," I said doubtfully.

But of course Baba loved a challenge. "Stop and turn, with your back to me," he said. "Now fall backward. Don't worry, I'll catch you."

He saw me hesitate. "Go ahead," he urged.

I took a deep breath and let myself fall backward. Baba caught me and said, "Do that again." I did, and again he caught me. "It got easier the second time, didn't it?"

"Yes," I said.

"And if we did it ten more times, you'd trust me completely?" he asked.

"I think so," I said. "I could still be a little nervous that you might trick me or get tired and miss."

"Well, all your soul wants is the same chance you gave me," said Baba. "Doubt if you like, but when you can, trust your soul to help you get something you really want. Once you get used to trusting, do it over and over. Eventually you will have no doubt at all."

"But there's always a bit of doubt," I pointed out.

"Really?" said Baba. "We were talking. Do you ever have the slightest doubt you'll get air?"

"No."

"That's because breathing is part of you," he said. "So is your soul. When you trust spirit, you are just trusting yourself. Give it a try. In time you will see that there is no more need for doubt."

WHAT I LEARNED

Why should you trust your soul? That's a big question, because most people don't. They may pray for something they really want, and when the prayer isn't answered, they put their trust somewhere else. But Baba taught me that I could ask my soul for things and trust that it would provide. He gave me some small steps as a start:

1. Think of the color red. Can you see it? You had no trouble getting your mind to see red, did you? It was automatic. Likewise, you will trust your soul more if you realize that it is automatic—you don't have to force it to listen to you.
2. Imagine that you take a bird out of its cage and throw it into the air. Can you trust it to fly back to you? Would it make a difference if the bird was a homing pigeon? Of course it would, because a homing pigeon has been trained to return. Likewise, you will trust your soul more as you train yourself to return to it again and again.
3. If a bear goes into a cave to hibernate, can you trust that it will come out next spring? Yes, because nature

has arranged that the bear obeys the timing of the seasons. Likewise, you will trust your soul more when you learn that there is a right time for everything it does.

4. If your mother puts dinner on the table and tells you to make sure the dog doesn't get it, what should you do? You could sit in the kitchen and watch the food all day. Or you could put it away on a shelf so that the dog can't reach it. Likewise, if you ask your soul for something, you don't have to watch out every minute to see what it does. You can put your wish away in a safe place and trust.

5. Imagine that some prisoners are in jail and the door is left open. Can you trust them to stay inside? No, because they naturally want to be free. Likewise, your soul wants you to be free, and if any opportunity arises to give you more freedom, you can trust your soul to take it.

Trust in the soul doesn't develop all at once. One wish isn't a good test, or even two or three. Baba taught me that I had to trust my soul a little more every day. Keep asking it to take you to that high place where visions become reality. Your soul is already there, and it will take you to the peak if you trust it to.

A Tale of Ups and Downs

When I'm with you, I feel as if anything is possible," I said. "I think my future will be exciting, and that wasn't true before. I'm different." Baba and I had retreated to a patch of woods near the village. We stayed out of sight while the kids came back from lunch.

"But you may have a downfall sometime—everyone does," said Baba. "Then you'll go back to how you were. It's human nature."

"I'd try to be better than that," I said.

"Would you?"

Smiling, he handed me the last of the chapati, flatbread wrapped around curry, just like the first day. "Handling ups and downs is hard for everyone. Make yourself comfortable and try not to doze while I tell you a little story."

Eating lunch hadn't made Baba the least bit sleepy, so while I curled up under the tree, he told me a tale of ups and downs:

Once there was a man who loved two things above

everything else in the world. One was his son and the other was a pony. One morning, however, the man awoke to find that the pony had run away. A search party was mounted, but the pony was nowhere to be found.

"You must feel terrible," a neighbor said when he heard the news.

But the man looked calm. "It's not over," he murmured.

The next day the man woke up, and not only had the pony returned, but with him came a magnificent white stallion. When he heard the news, his neighbor said, "You must be overjoyed. You have your pony and a new horse that's twice as beautiful."

But the man looked calm and said, "It isn't over."

The next day when his son was out riding the white stallion, he fell off and broke his leg. As the boy was carried into the house moaning with pain the neighbor said, "What a terrible accident. How much you must be suffering to see your poor son hurt."

But the man looked calm and said, "It's not over."

The next day the army came. They were taking away every able-bodied young man to go to war, but when they saw that the man's son was laid up with a broken leg, the soldiers went away and left him behind. The neighbor rushed over and said, "How fortunate you are. Every young man has to go to war except your son."

But the man only shrugged. "It's never over," he said.

Baba looked at me when he finished. "That story was a

parable. The neighbor stands for the mind, the father stands for the soul. The mind will always become panicky over life's ups and downs. But ups and downs never end; that's just the nature of life. Today cannot promise what tomorrow will bring.

"When everything else changes, your soul doesn't," said Baba. "It isn't here to change. It's here to prove that there's a part of you that is ever constant. Sailors were once terrified to go far out to sea, until they discovered the North Star. With just one star that was constant, they could sail to distant lands without fear. The next time you see that star, remind yourself that whatever worries your mind may have, your soul will never move or change."

Baba had more to tell me, but I couldn't hold my eyes open. The sweet smell of the grass under my head is the last thing I remember. That and Baba sitting so quietly that it was easy to imagine that he would never change either.

WHAT I LEARNED

This lesson was about balance. In Baba's tale about the pony the neighbor gets sad when anything goes wrong and happy when anything goes right. Change is all he knows. But the father stands back and takes everything in. He has a bigger view, and so he's able to be calm and steady. He's found a balance.

Nature is all about balance. Look at a tree. Its leaves sway with every little breeze, while the trunk stands totally strong and firm. Your mind is like that. Thousands of thoughts flicker through it, yet you have a core of yourself that holds firm, no matter what. Baba wanted me to jump in and go with the flow. But he also wanted me to be strong enough to hold up in a storm. So I learned not to be excited just because everyone else is. I learned to value a friend who can keep cool in a crisis. I learned to sit still and wait to see what comes next.

These sound like little things, but your soul does them. It keeps tender care over you, rarely making itself noticed. In its stillness it is saying, *I am always here for you, no matter what.*

"What Do I Need?"

A ll right, back you go," said Baba. We had waited until everyone returned from the village, and then he took me to the door of my school again.

"Really? I thought I was staying with you," I said. I couldn't hide my disappointment.

"I'll be back when the skies are right," Baba said mysteriously. He turned without another word and walked away, so I had no choice but to scramble back inside. All through math and history I thought about Baba. When the final bell rang, I rushed outside to see if he was waiting for me. But he wasn't, and as for the sky, it had started to rain.

At first the rain was light, so I decided to chance it and run home. Five minutes later the clouds turned black, and water came down in buckets.

"Nasty weather," a familiar voice said. I turned around and there was Baba, standing in the middle of the muddy road.

"Where did you come from?" I asked, wiping at the

rivulets that were cascading down my forehead.

"Technicalities," he said. "Your training is too important to waste on technicalities. Here, I brought you two things, but you can have only one. It's up to you."

He held out a folded umbrella in one hand and a chocolate bar in the other.

"The umbrella," I said without hesitation, grabbing it from his hand. I opened it, Baba ducked under with me, and the two of us started down the road again. But now the clouds crackled with lightning. One bolt struck so close by in the woods that it made me jump.

"It's getting nastier," said Baba. "But I can give you one of two things. Either this new pocketknife"—he was holding one in his hand—"or shelter from the storm."

"Shelter!" I shouted as the wind grew into a howling gale.

We rounded the next bend, and among the trees I spied a small cabin. Baba and I made a run for it, and a minute later we were safe inside. I was so cold and wet that I began to shiver all over.

"I wish there was some firewood or a heater," I grumbled.

"I can offer you one of two things," said Baba again. He held out a fluffy white towel in one hand and a shiny silver ring in the other.

"Towel," I said, although not as fast as before. I didn't really want a silver ring, but this one looked like it might be valuable.

As I dried myself off Baba said, "The soul does what you just did. It pays attention to what you really need. Today you needed an umbrella, a safe place, and a towel more than you needed a candy bar, a new pocketknife, or a silver ring. It's easy to want lots of things—who doesn't? But to know that your soul is working on just what you need—now, that's a rare thing indeed."

WHAT I LEARNED

If you ask yourself "What do I need?" the answer may seem simple. Maybe you need supper because you're hungry, or a little peace and quiet so that you can do your schoolwork. But the soul thinks about needs that you can't see. Some lie far ahead in the future, for example. On the material level DNA also works that way. It knows that a baby needs two sets of teeth, first the baby teeth and then the adult set. It isn't left to each baby to decide (not that it could), because nature has provided what's necessary in advance.

Just as DNA has knowledge of the future, so does your soul. Baba taught me that every life unfolds from stage to stage. What I needed at fifteen wasn't what I would need when I grew up and had a family. Yet compared to DNA, what the soul must plan is a thousand times more complicated because every word, thought, and action counts as a life unfolds. Your soul's knowledge applies to you alone, not to anyone else. DNA grows baby teeth for every child, while the soul must plan one unique life at a time.

So, what do you need? You must stay tuned in and find out. If one destiny fit everybody, each kid would be equally smart, equally popular, and equally athletic. Don't feel deprived if you think you don't have enough of something, because your soul is helping you to assemble a life that no one else will lead except you. One day your attention may be caught by a frog on the edge of a pond because you are meant to be a biologist, while your friend may notice only the water because he is meant to follow the sea.

The tiny things you notice and the tiny things you wish for work together. Bit by bit you are fitting together a thousand pieces of a puzzle, and when it is finally assembled, the whole will be you. Baba taught me to trust that I am unique and that my soul knows exactly what makes me perfect in my own way. The next time you feel disappointed that you didn't get what you wanted, remember that what you really want is matched by your soul to what you really need.

Your Time Is Coming

The rain ended, and Baba walked with me as I made my way home. When my house was in sight, he said, "I've found something for you."

"You did?" I thought I had kept my eye on him the whole time. But now he was holding out a bare twig. From one end dangled a single dead leaf, curled up and brown. Then I looked closer. It wasn't a leaf at all.

"A chrysalis," I said. "When will it hatch?"

At that moment the chrysalis quivered and a small, jagged slit opened on one side. Within minutes a butterfly was going to be born.

"Hold it carefully while I tell you something from a long time ago," said Baba. "Something that happened to me." I gingerly took the twig from his hand and watched it tremble while Baba began his story.

"One day when I was a boy, my father brought home a twig exactly like that one. He tied it to a low bush outside our door. I had never seen a butterfly emerge from its cocoon, and every day I woke up with excitement, thinking that today would be the day.

"Two weeks passed, and when I came out one morning to see the end of the twig trembling, just as it is now, I was beside myself with impatience. Soon a dark insect head appeared, then with great struggle, a body. The new butterfly was very weak. Being born had totally exhausted it.

"I watched as it clung to the twig, so spent that it couldn't unfurl its wings. They were soggy and crumpled, like wadded tissue paper. Taking pity on the poor creature, I blew on its wings to dry them. I blew and blew, and then something awful happened. I blew so hard that one wing tore."

"What did you do?" I asked, seeing the crippled wing in my mind's eye.

"There was nothing to do," said Baba. "I had to watch the torn wing dry out, and the butterfly limped away. It could barely fly."

We both were quiet for a moment before Baba said, "I didn't tell you that story to make you sad. It taught me something I never forgot. All things come in their own good time. Nature assigns a time for the butterfly to unfold its wings, and no one, not the most mighty emperor, has ever forced a butterfly to be born faster. Look at a rosebud as it unfolds into a beautiful flower. No power on Earth can make it open faster either. Nature knows its own best time."

"Does it know my best time?" I asked.

"Yes," said Baba. "Your soul knows when your time is coming, and it leads you step by step. In this way you fit perfectly into God's plan."

Baba's voice, which was always so calm, was filled with passion now. "Every small breath you take has its time, but so do the great events of your life. Your soul knows the end of the journey, but it will make every step a blessing along the way."

I felt a shiver run down my spine, because I'd never thought my life could have great events in it.

"Everyone's does," said Baba, reading my thoughts. "Every step you take with your soul is a great event, because through you life itself, as far as the most distant galaxy, is finding a new expression. Your next thought is as great as the birth of a star, as great as what you hold in your hand."

I had looked away from the twig and missed the butterfly's crawling out of its chrysalis. Now it was free, hanging upside down from the twig. The creature looked so weak and helpless that I knew why Baba had taken pity on it as a boy.

"It may look weak," said Baba. "But life has repeated this moment for millions upon millions of years. Ages have come and gone, yet nothing has stopped these fragile wings from unfolding."

We sat quietly and watched as the crumpled, damp

wings stiffened bit by bit. The butterfly twitched them over and over, and like magic sails they opened until they were ten times bigger than they started out. The dull brown color turned to the most sparkling blue. Finally the butterfly seemed to know that it was ready, because instead of twitching its wings, it flapped them. Its body was carried up in the air, and after a minute it was gone.

A mighty speck of life had just joined the cosmos.

WHAT I LEARNED

Baba convinced me that my soul knows how I feel and what I want. It knows the great events that will take place in my life. All these things are part of how a caterpillar turns into a butterfly. Imagine what it experiences. One day a caterpillar is chewing on a leaf, just like every other day, and it has this thought, *Maybe I'll weave some threads.*

It's never had such a thought before, but suddenly this idea is so strong that it weaves threads all around itself.

Now that I'm in here, I'm getting sleepy, it thinks. Everything becomes still inside. The caterpillar doesn't want to eat anymore; it doesn't even want to see daylight. Down it sinks into a kind of sleep, and then what happens? Every single cell in its body shifts and grows a new shape. At one point the old caterpillar is little more than a shapeless, soupy blob, and then out of nowhere a new body takes form.

Finally the caterpillar feels the impulse to wake up. *I*

don't want to be in here, it thinks. So it pokes and shoves and chews its way through the threads it has woven. All it wants is to see the light of day, and once it is hanging in the sun, it has an urge to twitch. It doesn't know it has wings; it doesn't even know what wings are. But in a minute or two all it wants to do is fly—without lessons!

Now, here's the big question: Can you grow in your own way with such perfect timing? Can you discover that you are unfolding into surprising stages you never expected? The soul is where the future stores its biggest surprises. Your DNA already contains a blueprint for your body to grow, which is amazing enough. When a baby begins as a single cell in its mother's womb, that cell already knows when the baby will grow its first tooth, when it will focus its eyes, grip with its hands, and learn to balance so that it can walk. Before a baby sees the world for the first time, its DNA knows that one day the same person will have gray hair. A whole life span is compressed into a speck thousands of times smaller than the period at the end of this sentence.

Your soul knows as much about your mind and heart as DNA knows about your body. It stores everything in its secret vault, every desire you might have. You aren't a puppet, though. You have choices, thousands of them every day. You can choose to tap into the most powerful force in the universe. That's what your soul is waiting for. The biggest event in anyone's life is when you make the cosmic connection, and Baba was about to show me just how it's done.

Day Three

What Is the Supreme Force in the Universe?

Alchemy

For a long time I didn't see Baba again. I looked for him under his favorite tree, but weeks passed and he wasn't there. I knew he was a wanderer. He didn't actually live under the tree but only rested until he felt the urge to roam. Summer came, and I gave up looking. I found myself thinking a lot. I would retreat to the cabin that Baba had found during the storm. It was perfectly hidden in the green gloom of the woods by its thick layer of vines.

I arrived one day to hear somebody laughing inside. And the laugh sounded like it could be only one person's.

"Baba!" When I threw open the door, he was standing in the middle of the cramped little hut dressed in his immaculate white clothes, exactly as before. "What were you laughing about?" I asked.

"A cosmic joke, which I'll tell you later," he said. Whatever that meant, I had a lot to tell him and a lot to ask, but Baba didn't let me do either. "So your third day begins," he announced.

"Perhaps I forgot to tell you, but I practice alchemy, the science of changing lead to gold. Only, that's too easy. I prefer the real alchemy, the kind that will work on people."

"Does that exist?" I asked.

"It must. It's working on you," he said. "You're changing before my eyes, and no wonder: I've unleashed a force, the supreme force in the universe, in fact."

"And what is that?" I asked.

"Love."

I could feel myself blushing; I didn't know what to say. Baba didn't laugh at my embarrassment, but said, "If I just loved you like a grandfather or a favorite uncle, you would flourish. Love is like fertilizer to the heart—it makes it grow and reach for the sun. But I am talking about something cosmic, a force that is much more powerful than family love or even romantic love.

"This reminds me of a story I heard when I was your age," said Baba, who then told me the following tale:

Once there was a man who loved God so much that he left home to live inside a temple. In India, God can be either father or mother. This man loved the Mother God more than anything else in the world, and so he spent every day arranging flowers on her altar and praying to her statue. He always went around wearing a dreamy smile, and people used to argue behind his back, some claiming that he was amazingly devoted, and others scoffing that he was more than a bit touched in the head.

One day the highest priest in that part of the country stopped by the temple, which was on the banks of a river. Stepping off his boat, he stumbled across the devotee. "You are said to worship the Divine Mother every day," said the priest.

"Yes," said the devotee, who was nervous and shy before such a great man.

"Do you know the proper prayers?" the priest sternly asked.

"No, I sing to Mother with the words that are in my heart," the devotee said.

The priest frowned. "Do you know the proper rituals and sacrifices?"

"No, I was never taught them," admitted the devotee, who was getting more nervous by the minute.

The high priest said, "I am worried about you. Sit with me and I will teach you the proper way to worship God."

So they sat together, and even though the devotee was slow and uneducated, after a while the priest was satisfied that he had taught him the correct way to worship. The day ended, and the priest got into his boat to sail back down the river. He was a hundred yards from shore when he heard the whole crew shouting.

"What's the commotion?" the priest said irritably.

Then he saw the devotee, who was walking over the water toward the boat. He came up to it, and in a humble voice he said, "I'm so sorry, but could you teach me the right way to pray again? I think I forgot."

But the high priest had fallen to his knees in awe before a true lover of God.

"That story is about what love can do when it is a cosmic force," said Baba. "Nothing in the universe is more powerful, and yet if you look inside, the same force is within you at this very moment."

WHAT I LEARNED

Can love really transform human nature, the way the ancient alchemists tried to turn lead into gold? Baba wanted to prove that it could. For him, love is a force that flows through everyone and everything. Many years later I came across a wonderful experiment that applies here. It involved a group of rabbits in a laboratory. They were kept in cages, and instead of eating lettuce and carrots, these rabbits were fed an extremely unhealthy diet to see if they would develop high cholesterol and hardened arteries, just as human subjects do when their diet is extremely unhealthy.

In time the rabbits became sick, as the researchers had expected—all but one group, and no one could understand why, because this group was eating the same diet as all the others. Then it was discovered that something different was happening to them. One of the college students assigned to feed this group of rabbits used to stroke and cuddle them before they were fed. The experimenters were forced to see that love, in the form of touching and caring, can actually change the body's chemistry.

I've never forgotten this experiment, but as a child I already knew a saying, "If you give nectar to an angry man, he will turn it into poison, and if you give poison to an enlightened man, he will turn it into nectar." So it wasn't hard for me to believe Baba when he said that love is more than a feeling. Love has the power to create change. What is it that people really want to change?

They want to be healed. This means in both mind and body, because life hurts us in both ways.

They want to feel safe. This means living without fear and knowing that you are accepted.

They want to expand. This means feeling more free, not having that suffocating feeling of being trapped or closed in.

They want to be inspired to do great and wondrous deeds. I don't have to explain this—why else does Hollywood make billions of dollars a year? Even the fantasy of great and wondrous deeds makes us go back for more.

As you look at yourself right now can you create these changes? Nobody can, not on their own just by thinking. You need true alchemy. You must release the same flow of love that was given to the rabbits. Baba taught me that alchemy comes from inside. People spend a lot of time looking for all kinds of outside solutions. They move, they change jobs and get new friends, they forget their troubles with games and sports and movies. They aren't thinking about love, however; the supreme power in the universe has been overlooked. The first thing Baba wanted me to know is that I should never overlook love again.

The Boy Who Needed Love

Baba had been standing still when suddenly, true to his habit, he moved quickly out the cabin door, heading straight for the road. I ran after him, thinking he was going to the village, but after a few moments he stopped. We had come across some boys up ahead.

"Take a look," he said.

I knew them all. Four boys from school who were kicking down the road on a summer day. They needed diversion, and at that moment they'd found something promising, because one of the boys was shouting, "No way! Go home, Stinky."

"What are we looking at?" I asked. Baba was paying close attention to the boy they were picking on.

"Someone in dire need of an alchemist," he said.

Jimmy Stinky? I thought. His real name was Jimmy Starkey, which made him unpopular to begin with because he had an Indian mother and a British father. He was the kid who forever got teased. Jimmy was wiry and small for his age. Somebody—probably his dad—had told him that he had to try and fit in. So every Saturday, like clockwork, Jimmy showed up to give it another try. This time he held out a new cricket ball. Indian boys are probably even more crazy for cricket than for soccer.

"Where'd you get that ball?" one of the other boys said. "Hand it over." Jimmy hesitated. "What's wrong, you afraid we'll take it?"

"We just want to see your ball, Stinky. What's wrong with that?" another boy chimed in.

"Okay," Jimmy said doubtfully. He handed the ball to the first boy, who started tossing it up and down. "My dad bought it, for all of us," Jimmy said. He was actually sounding hopeful.

"Please, Baba, let's go," I said. It made me uncomfortable to watch; I had been one of Jimmy's tormentors, and if Baba hadn't been there, my attitude would have been just like his present tormentors'. But Baba wouldn't budge.

I don't have to tell you how this scene was playing out. After they began tossing his ball around, the three boys wouldn't throw it to Jimmy; then he wanted it back, but they wouldn't give it to him; then they threw it into a ditch and walked away laughing.

"I'm watching him," said Baba. "I'm feeling his misery, but I can also feel his tormentors, who are happy and satisfied with how they treated him. It's a little drama about human nature, isn't it?" Jimmy was now in the ditch by the side of the road trying to find his lost ball in the weeds.

I didn't want to get involved at all. Jimmy found his ball in the muddy ditch, and when we passed him, he hung his head while I looked the other way. Baba let me walk down the road at my own slow pace. I couldn't get Jimmy out of my mind, and more than once I wanted to turn and run after him.

"And what would you do if you caught up with him?" Baba asked.

"I'd tell him I was sorry," I said.

"What if he didn't want to listen?" Baba asked.

"I'd try and convince him."

"How?"

I didn't like being interrogated. I had stood by and watched while Jimmy was ragged without mercy. There was no good reason why he should trust me. I did have an idea, though. "I'd ask him if he wanted to practice pitching and batting with me. He's really lousy at cricket," I said.

Baba shook his head. "Once a dog's been beaten, it's hard to make him see your hand holding anything but a stick."

Baba had never talked so grimly before, and I wondered why he was trying to make me feel even guiltier.

"Guilt is pointless," he said impatiently. "It adds more

pain when what you want is less. There are subtle ways to show Jimmy that you've changed inside. Let me show you."

Baba would have made a great actor, because in an instant he changed before my eyes. He stiffened and crossed his arms like a policeman confronting a guilty criminal. His eyes looked right through me, and his body tightened into a rigid pillar. "How do I look?" he said.

"Pretty scary."

"And how do I look now?"

Without so much as a moment's hesitation he changed again. His body softened, the sternness in his face melted, and I saw myself reflected in his eyes just as I did in my mother's when I came home from boarding school.

"That's amazing," I said.

"The soul finds many ways to express what is true about you," said Baba. "Through your body language, your tone of voice, the look in your eyes, the whole sense you give off of being tense or relaxed."

"I never notice those things," I said.

"Oh, we all notice, but we pretend not to," said Baba. "That's what is so amazing about this particular secret weapon. It's out in plain sight, yet it still remains a secret."

WHAT I LEARNED

This lesson is about bonding, which doesn't happen in what you do or say or think. The moment an animal is born, it bonds with the first living creature it sees. You can hatch baby geese, for example, away from their mother, and if a man is watching them emerge from the shell, they will follow him for the rest of their early life as if he were their mother. A human baby learns to recognize its mother's smile within a few hours of being born, and soon the baby's eyes will go to that face and watch it over any other face. Mother and child must bond, for that is how the baby's brain develops, by paying attention to when the mother smiles or frowns. Your whole sense of who you are originally came from watching your mother's reactions in those first days of life.

Probably the most fascinating story I've heard about bonding has to do with autistic children. Autism is a condition that causes babies to go inside themselves and pay no attention to the outside world. Such babies show no interest in other people. They blank out music and television. It is sad to see an autistic child spend an entire day sitting in one place bobbing back and forth, a prisoner in a silent world.

These children were considered unreachable for a long time, and then some wonderful exceptions showed up. In one case an autistic boy from India began to write beautiful poetry even though he could barely speak. In another case a father got down on the floor and imitated all the strange twitches and twiddles that his son made, and after many months the son started paying attention—

he came out of his inner world and began to show signs of life.

In other words, someone bonded with these kids, silently saying, *I am here for you.* And in one case an autistic boy who had shown barely any interest in the outside world suddenly began to write and do math, skills he had learned all by himself. When asked how he had done that, he tapped out a message with one finger on his alphabet board: "I've been listening." I felt a lump in my throat when I heard that story, because I suddenly knew that a child inside us is always listening, no matter what we see on the outside.

Autism is related to a brain disorder, a disease, but even in normal people the power of bonding is amazing. I can think of a famous moment in World War I when the enemy troops had been facing each other from the trenches for years, at great cost of life, without either side advancing so much as half a mile. Christmas Eve arrived, and on either side the soldiers emerged from the trenches to sing carols. The feelings of war fell away for that magical moment, and although this happened in several places on the front lines, in one particular place many soldiers reported seeing a mysterious light hovering over the trenches, a light that some identified as an angel.

Is this possible? Baba taught me that I would never know the power of love until I began to bond, because love can't flow when it is trapped inside one person.

Bonding comes down to specific things you can do in every relationship you have, either at home or with friends:

Look in the other person's eyes with acceptance.

Show that you understand their point of view.

Don't rush to make your point of view seem right.

Show respect in every situation, even when you feel angry and argue. Both sides of an argument need to be able to walk away feeling respected.

Be willing to compromise.

Do your best to feel what the other person feels. Put yourself in their position.

If you are in a bad mood, tell the other person that it is not their fault.

Give the other person the gift of approval, smiles, and laughter.

Make some sort of physical contact if it is appropriate, showing with a light touch on the shoulders, a hug, or shaking hands that you feel close.

Show in your body language that you feel relaxed around the other person. Relaxed body language means that your arms and legs aren't crossed; your shoulders are lowered; you face them directly, not turning to one side; and your facial muscles are relaxed.

Bonding comes naturally when your heart opens. If you want to know the one thing, however, that breaks down bad feelings, it is respect. If you show respect for how someone else feels, you can bond even though you disagree. Your respect says, *I accept you as a person equal to me,* and although we often say that in words, meaning it from the soul is ten times more important.

The Secret of Attraction

Is there a girl you're really attracted to?" asked Baba. What a question! The truth is that I had never had a girlfriend. We were very innocent in India back then. Kids barely held hands on a first date, even late in high school. I didn't know one boy who had gotten his first kiss. Most of the time we just watched girls from afar.

"Then tell me this," said Baba when I didn't answer. "Why are boys and girls attracted to each other?"

"It just happens," I said. "It's physical." I couldn't believe we were going into this topic.

At least one of us looked comfortable. Baba said, "Physical attraction just happens, yes. But it masks something deeper. This is another mystery of the soul, and you should know about it."

Baba lay back and stared up through the leaves gently swaying in a calm breeze. Flickers of sunlight played over his wrinkled face, and his expression looked so deep and far away that he could have been thinking about some girl of his own—a lost love, perhaps?

"I'm not thinking of a person," he said, picking up my thoughts. "I'm thinking of how to show you something. Ah!"

He sat up with a gleam in his eye. "Imagine that you've just met a beautiful girl. The two of you are attracted to each other, and you begin to see her every day. One day you notice that she's wearing a necklace with a shiny stone pendant. 'What's that?' you ask. She doesn't seem to hear your question, because she keeps talking about something else.

"For some reason that shiny stone sticks in your mind. The next time you see her, you say, 'Oh, you're wearing it again.' 'It's nothing,' she says, and starts talking about something else. Only now the stone looks a little bigger and shinier.

"Now your curiosity is piqued, so you return the next day, and the stone has gotten very large and shiny. *What if it's a diamond?* you think. *Maybe she's wearing a diamond that's so valuable she doesn't want to tell me about it.*

"Can you imagine how this story will turn out?" Baba asked.

"She never tells?" I said doubtfully.

"That's right. But the diamond just keeps getting bigger and bigger in your eyes, until you are sure it must be the most precious jewel on earth. That's how attraction grows into deep love. You have to make only one little change."

Baba tapped me on the chest. "The diamond is in there. You'll never see it and she will never talk about it, but when you are attracted to a girl—or when a girl is attracted to a boy—love shows you something precious that you can't stop wondering about."

WHAT I LEARNED

It's easy to be attracted to somebody; it's even easy to fall in love. But Baba wanted me to go deeper. Loving someone else for the spirit inside is like finding a precious jewel that only grows more fascinating. The steps on this path are the same as Baba outlined:

> *You notice something special that catches your eye.*
> *You become intrigued.*
> *The thing you notice grows in your eyes.*
> *As it grows it becomes more and more special—you begin*
> *to find it precious.*

So, what could this mysterious thing be that attracts you and then turns into a diamond? Everyone could come up with a different answer, but the following three things are at the top of my list.

KINDNESS

There is something incredibly touching when you find a kind person. Kindness comes so naturally to them that they don't notice it, because they aren't *trying* to be kind. You know what it's like to force yourself to "do the right thing" when you don't want to. I'm sure you've done the right thing by visiting a sick patient in the hospital or spending time with an older relative or volunteering for a good cause. Kindness doesn't always come easily, but when it does, the person whose heart is naturally kind is able to fascinate me year after year. My love never grows old. Kindness can also be called courtesy of the heart.

COMPASSION

Compassion is kindness carried a step further. That makes it even more rare. Most people can stop to give spare change to a homeless person, but few would ask if that person needed medical help or a hot meal and then see that he got it. When I see compassion in someone's eyes, I am reminded of a parable about some horsemen crossing a stream.

They call for the ferryman, who shouts across the stream, "How many of you are there?"

One of the horsemen says, "Let me count." He counts and shouts back, "There are nine of us."

"Really?" the ferryman calls. "I counted ten. Count again."

So the horseman does, and again he shouts that there are nine. The ferryman takes his boat across. "What's the matter with you?" he says in exasperation. "Every time you count, you get nine because you forget to count yourself."

The horseman looks confused. "I'm supposed to count myself?" he says.

Compassionate people are exactly like that. They are so selfless that they forget to count themselves. In our society forgetting to count yourself can make you seem foolish or naive, but to me it's one of the most lovable qualities anyone can possess.

PEACE

This is another rare quality to find, because most people are at peace only when their surroundings are peaceful. It's not hard to be at peace when you come from a happy, contented home and have happy and contented friends. But some people can be at peace anywhere, even on a battlefield. The ancient philosopher Socrates served in the army as a young man, and everyone around him was amazed by his ability to be in danger and yet show complete calm. The same is true of the world's saints and sages. The reason that wisdom and peace go together is that you have to look deep to get past all the reasons for *not* being peaceful. These reasons are everywhere. People feel angry or afraid, they worry that things will fall apart or they worry that things have *already* fallen apart—the list never ends. But there is only one reason to be at peace, and that's because your soul is. Peaceful people seem to show you their soul, and that makes them fascinating without end.

I could add a lot more qualities to this list. I've been attracted to people because they are courageous or completely honest or truly wise about human nature, or they just have a joyful *something* in their eyes. Find the hidden jewel in every person and keep noticing it every day. I promise that it will become the most precious diamond on Earth.

Shopping for People

As soon as we reached the village, I ran for the vendor who sold sugarcane juice. In India back then you couldn't buy sodas, at least not in the countryside. Instead a special machine was set up at a vendor's stall that squeezed fresh chunks of sugarcane, and the sweet juice was poured over ice to make a cool drink.

"Want one?" I asked Baba while mine was being squeezed.

But he was too busy looking around at the marketplace with all its shops and stalls. He took in the scene casually, but there was X-ray vision behind his gaze.

"A lot of people are out shopping today," he remarked. That wasn't unusual; housewives came to the stalls every day to get food to cook, and everyone had to come here to buy the small necessities.

"But some of them are shopping for people," Baba said. "See?" He pointed to a small crowd just ahead of us. It was made up of four or five teenage girls sitting together near the covered bazaar. A few yards away a similar group of boys were huddled together, keeping their distance but checking out everything the girls were doing. I didn't recognize any from my school.

"Here," said Baba. He opened his hand, and in it was a hundred-rupee note. "Let's put you on the market." I can't tell you how many dollars a hundred rupees was back then, but I'd never seen such a large bill. Baba folded it and put it in my shirt pocket.

"What do you want me to spend it on?" I asked.

"Don't spend it. Just walk around and be noticed." Baba had arranged the note so that one end stuck out in plain sight.

"I can't walk around with money showing," I said.

"But that's the experiment. I want you to get into the game of people-shopping. It will only be for an hour." Baba kept insisting. I felt very uneasy, but in the end I agreed to do it for half an hour.

It was the longest half hour of my life. Everyone stared in curiosity to see a kid with that kind of money sticking out of his pocket. The group of girls were the worst. They erupted in giggles when they saw me coming, and after I passed, I overheard them whispering. The boys glared at me as if I had grabbed their turf, and I glared back. Anyway, the whole thing was nerve racking, and I was glad to get back to Baba.

I tore the money from my pocket and almost threw it back at him. "That was horrible!"

"Why? For half an hour you were the best thing going," he said with mock seriousness. "You should be happy."

"It had nothing to do with me, it was just the money they saw." I was calming down only a little.

"Now you understand the trouble love gets into," said Baba, "when people mistake it for shopping. Those boys and girls are picky shoppers. They want only somebody who looks nice and feels nice and maybe smells nice, like a new car."

"Isn't that being a little cynical?" I said.

Baba shook his head. "Ask the ones who don't get picked."

I couldn't argue with that. As every kid knows, getting picked depends a lot on the same things that go into picking a new car—because it's cool or makes the buyer feel important and successful—while the cars that don't get picked feel like rejects even before someone rejects them.

I said, "How can you stop boys from checking out girls and girls from checking out boys?"

"I don't want to. But what are they seeing?" Baba said. "Nobody saw you just now; they saw what you had on display. The worst thing about being on display is that you can't be yourself."

"Nobody walks around showing their money," I pointed out.

"Maybe not the bills," said Baba. "But they show what

the money can buy, or how confident and cool it makes them feel. Love is the opposite of being on display. You show who you are. If you don't, you'll never be able to trust how others are relating to you. They could be acting approving or jealous or secretly hostile, yet none of these reactions are about you—they're about what meets the eye. Shopping for people is the worst way to find true love." Baba started chuckling to himself.

"What?" I said.

"I was just thinking how everything in the world of the soul comes down to not believing your eyes and believing only what can't be seen."

WHAT I LEARNED

I think this lesson speaks for itself. Then why is it so hard to remember? Everyone knows that you shouldn't judge by appearances. Nobody ever had a father and mother who said, "I want to give you some advice about falling in love. Pick only the coolest person you can find, and if they stop being cool, turn them in for a better model." Yet social life often revolves around shopping for people, just as Baba said. The heart value is pushed out of the way in favor of externals.

When you're a shopper, what do you usually look for first? Labels. A nice skirt is twice as nice if it has the right label. A basketball that says NBA feels like it has something special. So early on in life we become aware that we are wearing labels, and unfortunately, what others see first is often nothing but a set of labels. Who am I? You could list all my labels: my name, address, race, skin color, income bracket, college degrees. It took a lifetime to get all these labels, but only a few of them look very, very nice. Others are average, and one or two might make people say, "Oh, you know him, that Indian," or "You know him, that guy who's always giving his opinion." Inside, I don't feel like any of these labels, so I don't work hard at making people see the good ones. I want them to see me with no labels at all.

As Baba told me then, shopping is a terrible way to find love. When I am tempted to judge others by how they look or how much money they make or how important they are, I can stop myself with just one reminder: *This person is going to turn into what I see.*

I'm sure you've noticed this yourself. If somebody walks up to you with a thousand dollars sticking out of their pocket, automatically they become a flashy rich person. Someone who mistreated you two months ago can walk into the room today, and all you see is how much you resent them. Appearances are considered superficial, but actually they turn out to be extremely powerful because we buy into the judgments we make on the spot.

Just remember that making an impression goes both ways. Half the time you are looking at others, and half the time they are looking at you. You can walk down the hall at school, and no matter how you act, every single person looking at you will create their own impression of who you are. What this means is that working hard to create an impression is self-defeating. You can't make people see you the way you want them to.

You also have the same power, right this moment, to see any person in any way you choose. Use this power well. Don't make the same assumptions everyone around you is making. Be honest and open every time you look at anyone. Friends and enemies are created, not born, and the place where they are created is in your heart. The girl you might dislike has somebody else who loves her. So if you look with an open heart, you will find those same qualities. That's what it means to hold someone in your heart. You allow the bonding process to start naturally, and in time a stranger feels like part of you.

Looking in the Mirror

Do you think girls are mysterious?" Baba asked.
"Very mysterious," I said without hesitating a second. We were still walking around the village, with its bustle of animals and people.

"Do you know why?" he asked.

I grinned. "I guess I have my whole life ahead of me to figure it out."

But Baba was already fumbling for something in his pockets. "Here it is." He pulled out a small mirror and held it beside his face. "What do you see?"

"Is this a trick question? I see my face," I replied.

"Perfect! You get the point?"

I shook my head.

"Girls are mysterious because boys are looking for themselves and finding someone else instead."

"I don't know about that. I'm not looking for myself," I protested. "I'm looking for a girl I like."

"Just think about it. What do you see when you look in

113

a mirror? You see what you like and what you don't like. Mostly the latter, right? Mirrors show every flaw. I'm sure you spend the required hours before a mirror when nobody is looking."

"The witness refuses to answer," I said. Of course Baba was right.

"Nobody looks in the mirror to see themselves as they really are," Baba said. "They always look for an image. And that's true when boys look at girls or girls look at boys.

"The image you have of yourself holds power over you. It magnifies what you think is good and bad; it is filled with fantasies about the future and memories of the past. Which is why girls seem so mysterious. Boys don't realize that they are looking at their own dreams and fears."

I thought this was pretty interesting but at the same time pretty confusing. "Let's say I see a really attractive girl. I like her shape, the way she walks, her smile. How am I seeing myself?"

Baba shook his head. "You're seeing what you want for yourself. If you happened to be in a bad mood and wanted to pick a fight, you'd see in that same girl exactly what you needed to make an argument break out. The mirror is magical. It always shows us what we want to see."

Baba grew quiet and, I think, a little sad. "When people fall in love they should look beyond the image in the mirror," he said. "But that isn't easy. When you love an image, you are loving something stuck in your mind. Your soul has a different idea about love." Baba took the hand mirror and tilted it to the sun.

"See?" he said. "I can show you the sun's image, but if the sun appeared only in a mirror, it would have no power to nourish the planet. Love nourishes you when you look at it directly; it's just a pretty thing when you look at its reflection. Think about that."

WHAT I LEARNED

I did think about what Baba said, and the more I thought about it, I could see that everyone is putting up an image. Boys aren't really looking at girls, and girls aren't really looking at boys. Their images are looking at each other. What if a boy feels insecure? He may find a girl who is totally devoted, but in his mind she will talk to other boys too much, flirt when his back is turned, and give a hundred little causes for jealousy. That's how powerful a mental image can be. (Think of the millions of people who worship movie stars and pretend that the real person is incredibly glamorous off the screen, incredibly brave and romantic. In reality actors aren't different from ordinary people, but their image says they have to be.)

Only at the soul level is a real person looking for another real person. Deep down, the heart can't be fooled by images—not for long, at least. It understands that love has to be honest. When you love someone, you find the courage to say, "You are my mirror." You look into your beloved's eyes and accept what you see, including your own imperfections. If you do that, suddenly the imperfections don't seem so horrible. The secret is that you feel loved, and that feeling melts through the image in your mind.

It's incredibly stressful to live up to an image. Images strive to be perfect. Images are afraid to shatter; they have to stand apart and never show weakness. When you begin to see yourself honestly in the mirror of another person, a lot of that stress begins to fade away. It's such a relief. And when the image finally vanishes, love can relax and blend into the joy of another person's heart.

Good Versus Evil

Looking back, I think it's strange that I didn't ask Baba lots of things. Like, "Where do you come from? How did you learn so much, some kind of school?" I never really found out any facts about him at all. Maybe I didn't want him to be too real, with an ordinary life like everyone else's. I liked being in a world that was just Baba and me, at least for three days.

But there was one question that anybody would ask. "Baba, what about evil?" I said as we sat under our favorite tree, the old, twisted one by the side of the road. The village was behind us now, and the afternoon was drawing on. "A lot of people would claim that evil is just as powerful as love."

"True, they would," said Baba. He had his eyes closed as he sat in his cross-legged pose. "Evil is more visible than love. It leaves destruction in its path. Some destruction is necessary. Plants produce thousands of seeds for every one that grows; if they all survived, the whole planet would soon be choked to death.

"To be alive means that you are part of a cycle that destroys things. Take your fingernail and scrape it inside your cheek." Baba opened his eyes and watched while I did that. "You have destroyed hundreds of cells that were alive just a second ago," he said. "So destruction isn't always evil. Thousands of skin cells will die and slough off from your body this week, making way for a fresh layer of new skin."

"But destroying the life of others, that has to be evil," I said.

"Really? You probably crushed dozens of insects under your feet as you walked along, not thinking about them, and billions of germs are killed by your white blood cells every year. Is any of that evil?"

"It could be," I said doubtfully.

"Yes, depending on who is making the call," he said. "I'm sure the ants would rather be alive, and maybe even the germs—who knows what they think?"

"Then potentially there's evil everywhere," I said.

"You have to decide that for yourself," said Baba. "Evil is not absolute. It exists in the eyes of human beings, and we are very fickle, as you know. Yesterday's evil could be tomorrow's good."

Baba gave me an example. "What if we had met two hundred years ago? I'd see you walking down the road, and I'd say, 'How was your day?' You might say, 'Oh, the same as ever. I got up at four in the morning and was weaving a rug before dawn. I worked for eleven hours, but my master hit me with his stick only three or four times.'

"People used to live such a life without question, and some still do," Baba said. "Isn't it evil to beat children and work them to the bone? To us it is, but two hundred years ago such a life showed that a child was doing God's work."

"People do bad things," I insisted. "There's a constant battle between good and evil."

"Yes, but your soul doesn't join the fight," said Baba. "Its job is to make evil vanish without a fight."

"That's hard to believe," I said. "Evil doesn't just disappear."

"Of course it does. All the time," said Baba. "Imagine that you are three years old and you've lost your mother in the market. You're alone and terrified; you think she's never coming back. You might not even survive. Isn't that what evil feels like? Then she finds you again. Presto, the evil is gone."

"Because the kid was just imagining things," I said.

"And that's how your soul sees all evil," said Baba. "You think you know what's really, truly evil? You think you can tell the good guys from the bad guys? I envy you, because I can't. I am like the mother rushing to find her lost child. I know that you are frightened and alone, and I can't wait to show you that what you are so afraid of is only imagination."

WHAT I LEARNED

This was a radical lesson from Baba. He knew, and so did I, that millions of people think that evil is cosmic. They believe in the devil and pray not to fall into his clutches. The story of the Garden of Eden seems to tell us that human beings have already fallen into sin, so even an innocent baby is caught in a web of evil that isn't its fault.

How could Baba claim that evil is imaginary? Even if you have a soul, even if you go to heaven when you die, even if God loves all of us equally, don't a huge number of bad things still keep happening in the world? I have heard people use the words *bad, evil, wicked,* or *wrong* about all the following things:

Shoplifting
Robbing a bank
Mistreating children
Letting children do what they want
Skipping school
Killing somebody
Buying a lottery ticket
Betting all your money on the stock market
Going to war
Refusing to go to war and being against war

You can see that this is a tricky list: Some things on it don't seem evil at all to me; some things are so evil they are considered crimes or sins; other things are considered bad, but so are their opposites. In Victorian times children were beaten and disciplined harshly to develop "character," yet today the same practice would be called child abuse. Throughout history war has been called evil, but war resisters have also been considered criminals and traitors to their country.

So that's the first thing Baba wanted me to see. Evil is hard to pin down, and a lot depends on who is making the call. What about pain? Isn't it wrong to inflict pain on somebody? Yes, but running a marathon brings extreme pain; so does surgery, which saves lives. There isn't a cosmic force called evil; there are only situations where pain and suffering occur. Can these ever go away?

I believe they can. Human nature can change through love. It may happen slowly, but pain makes all of us want to find a better way to live. That's the second point Baba was making: If you see someone in pain, help it to disappear. The answer to the question, "Can I help?" comes in many forms:

When someone feels afraid and unsafe, help make them feel safe.

When someone has failed, make them see all the ways they already succeed and will succeed again.

When someone has lost a loved one, share their pain and grief, but know that life goes on, and no one is ever lost on the soul level.

When someone is overwhelmed by events, help them look inside to find a place of peace.

When someone feels physical pain and illness, offer comfort and love. Persuade them to find the best medical help possible, remembering that sometimes physical illness defeats the psychology, making it hard to seek help.

Life is always going to have both pleasure and pain in it. Don't set out to fill your life only with fun, because that's not realistic; don't call pain evil, because that's unrealistic too. The third thing Baba wanted me to know about good versus evil is that life is in balance, and balance works for the good of life everywhere. Imagine that you're Mother Earth. She has seen billions upon billions of creatures go through birth and death. She has witnessed destruction that swept away whole continents and all the animals that lived on them.

Is this cycle of birth and death evil? You could focus in on any given minute and see destruction, or you could stand back and see a glorious vision of life triumphing over all obstacles. I have a very personal story to tell about that. My father died very suddenly a few years ago; he was more than eighty and had led a full and happy life. But it was a shock not to have said good-bye, and when I flew to India for his funeral, I felt full of grief.

The day of the funeral came; it was bright and hot. I was part of a procession taking my father out of the house for the last rites, which in India include burning the body.

I looked around, and here's what I saw: Some people were crying, others looked peaceful and calm. Little children ran up to grab the flowers that fell as we passed. They were laughing and looked on this procession as a big, curious event. Strangers glanced our way for a second but paid little attention. A mother carried her baby across our path; an old man slept in a doorway in the sun.

Suddenly I realized something: *I am not in a funeral procession. I am in the procession of life.* All around me was the whole cycle of life, and instead of feeling grief, I suddenly felt very expanded and free. It's that same feeling, which can surprise you when you least expect it, that makes evil vanish. You realize that life is going to triumph, despite everything, and close to your soul a voice is saying, *I am life.* This voice is telling the truth. Goodness is eternal, evil is temporary.

What's the best answer to the problem of evil? Don't curse the darkness and struggle against it. Light a candle, because light automatically drives darkness away. It's not the good deeds you do that make you good, it's who you are. And who you are is a soul walking around in a body, not a body walking around hoping it has a soul. Once you link up with that eternal part of yourself, evil can no longer make you afraid.

Loving Yourself

It was getting close to dusk, a time when the whole world seen from the hillside started to fill with golden light. "Look," I once heard a traveler say. "The gods have come out to play." It was just like that. Every house and tree and cloud shimmered as the last heat waves rose in ripples from the valley.

"Our third day is ending," said Baba as we looked out over the view. "Now I'm going to tell you the most difficult thing about love. But don't laugh at me."

"Why would I laugh?" I said.

"Because I have a nursery rhyme for you, and you might think I'm being childish," he said.

"Or mystical. I know you, remember?"

"You think so?" Baba chuckled. "But you're right: Things are always more mystical with me than with other people. Sometimes even a nursery rhyme hides great wisdom. This one is Humpty Dumpty."

"Who sat on a wall and had a great fall?"

"Yes, him," said Baba. "But do you know why all the king's horses and all the king's men couldn't put him back together again? It's a riddle."

"Not about eggs," I said.

Baba shook his head. "If you go back in time, there have always been myths about a golden age, when peace reigned, everyone felt love for one another, and life was perfect. But that golden age fell apart, and everyone's been trying to figure out how to put it back together again."

"This is your theory of Humpty Dumpty?" I asked.

Baba smiled. "It's good to stretch." He sounded very definite. "What really fell apart was love. There was never a golden age, at least not as far as any historian can tell. But deep in the human heart a memory lingers of how love should be. It should extend to everyone; it should leave no cause for suffering. It should be innocent and bring joy every day.

"Can that kind of love be put back together again? Your soul thinks so. Now we come to the most important step, which is this: You must love yourself."

I said, "Why is that difficult? I love myself, at least I think I do."

"Really?" asked Baba. "Which self did you pick? There's you as a baby, you playing with paper dolls when you were three, you when you are angry or sad, you when you believe in yourself, and you when you don't. Which one are you going to love?"

He was trying to stump me, but I felt pretty confident. "Those aren't me anymore. I love the me who's right here, now."

"But he will be gone tomorrow, just as those others are gone. Then what?" asked Baba. "You see, the nursery rhyme is right. We're all trying to put ourselves back together from bits and pieces. But all the king's horses and all the king's men won't be able to do it."

Baba must have seen a downcast look on my face, because his voice softened. "Don't be dejected. When you met me in the cabin today, didn't I tell you that I was laughing at a cosmic joke?"

"Yes," I remembered. "And you promised to tell it to me."

"Well, now's the time. The cosmic joke is that Humpty Dumpty never fell and was never broken. The real you is perfectly loved and always will be. No evil or harm can ever come to that you, and when you find it, you will be laughing with joy and relief, just as I do."

WHAT I LEARNED

Loving yourself can be a good feeling that hits you when you are on top of the world and everything is going right. It can also be feeling like a good person who deserves the best out of life. But Baba had a more cosmic idea of loving yourself. He pointed me to the place where myths are born.

Every person has a mythic level. It lies deep in our imagination; it's where we go for heroes and the quests that heroes follow. Whether you pick a knight of the Round Table, Wonder Woman, Joan of Arc, Gandhi, or Abraham Lincoln isn't just a personal choice—you are connecting to your mythic level. "I always ask people to tell me who their heroes are," Baba said. "I can tell a great deal about someone's whole life from who they secretly want to be."

In fact, you may want to do that for yourself. Write down three people, real or imaginary, who are your heroes. Then list three qualities you admire in each one, such as courage or superpowers, deep wisdom or great sacrifice for humanity. Look at your list. Do you know what those nine qualities really are? They are a mission from the mythic level. Your soul wants you to perform this mission in your lifetime by displaying the qualities you listed. Since they come from the mythic level, each one is *in you,* planted like a seed for the future.

As the years unfold you will be given opportunities to learn each quality. People who admire courage are magnetized to situations that require bravery. People who admire wisdom will be magnetized to completely different situations. Never fear, your soul isn't going to forget your mission. And what about superheroes with supernormal powers? Every kid admires them, because what they really stand for isn't flying or turning invisible. They stand for freedom. A supernormal power is like a hint from the soul that you are more than human—you are a free spirit. If you want to love yourself, grasp every opportunity for growing into your own hero. We were born to be the heroes of our own story.

I cherish a story about two old men sitting together in a room waiting for a meal. One was considered very wise and had gained fame in many countries; the other was a visitor who had come to find out what this wisdom was all about. But the famous wise man didn't say anything particularly wise all day, and finally the visitor got frustrated.

"Forgive me," he said. "But I don't see how you and I are any different. You have shown me hospitality, but let's be honest. Aren't we just two old men sitting at a table waiting for our supper?"

"You are wrong," the wise man said. "You have spent your whole life guarding your own private world. It is made up of past memories and your many likes and dislikes. It is populated with a few people you love and is shut tight to anyone else. My inner world isn't like that. It is open to everyone. All may enter and are welcomed. When I look inside, love is all I see, so I have nothing to hide and nothing to guard."

I've returned to this little story many times over the years because it tells me that the place where love never fades is real. I believe this is the only vision worth living for.

Day Four

How Can I Change the World?

Chasing Rainbows

The next morning I didn't have to search for Baba anywhere. When I went down to the kitchen for breakfast I caught a glimpse of wispy white hair just peeking up over the windowsill. I ran out to greet him. He was sitting beside the back door looking at the sky as if waiting for something to happen.

"Baba, come inside and eat a bowl of rice," I said.

"Would I become more real if your parents saw me?" he asked.

"I know you're real. I don't need any proof," I protested.

"Then you're assuming too much," he said. "Most people think they're real but have never proved it to themselves." These may sound like weary words, but Baba looked as fresh as ever. If I had imagined him from stories about wizards, he wasn't one of the dour, glum ones.

He said, "I've thought of an excellent project for us today. We're going to chase a rainbow."

This sounded like something you'd say to a five-year-old, but I knew he had something else in mind, so I rushed back inside, stuffed some food in my pockets, and was back out the door in two minutes. Baba was still peering at the sky. "It doesn't look like rain," he said.

"Not much chance for a rainbow, then," I said. Baba had already started to stride away quickly in his usual fashion.

"We don't have to rely on chance," he said over his shoulder. "Not that much happens by chance."

Not when I'm with you, I thought. We walked down the road and then cut across a broad field, where it was cooler and more lush. "What do you think a rainbow is?" he asked.

"It's sunlight that has been bent by the raindrops. Each one acts like a tiny prism." I knew this from grade-school science.

"Or it's a little hint," said Baba.

"A hint about what?"

"How the universe was made," he said. "In a rainbow you can see the whole universe. What is the universe? Light and space. Some of that light has become matter, and some of that matter is water. So everything the universe is made of shines through a rainbow. Every particle in creation contains the whole."

We were still climbing the hill, going higher than we had anytime before. It was getting hard to hike and talk at the same time. "Then, we're actually chasing the universe?" I asked.

"In a way. But I think the hint that we're following is even bigger," said Baba, who gave no sign that he noticed how tired I was getting.

"What's bigger than the universe?" I asked. With every foot we climbed I saw that Baba was working himself into a better mood, and now he was wearing his *I know a secret* smile.

"Someone who can change the universe," Baba said.

"And who can do that?"

"You," he said. "Nobody else but you."

WHAT I LEARNED

A lot of the time spirituality is about the impossible, and this fourth day was no exception. I'm sure you've heard it said that youth is the most idealistic time of life. Kids want to change the world, and by the time they grow up, they realize that they can't. The world is just going to be the way it is, and there's nothing one person can do about it. Baba didn't subscribe to that belief. Yet he was very far from being a starry-eyed idealist. To him, changing the world is the most natural thing anyone can do. In fact, it's impossible *not* to change the world. So he went a step further and told me I could change the universe.

The secret is invisible, as always. Look at a distant galaxy whose light takes millions of years to get to Earth.

Do you feel far away from that galaxy? Your eyes say that you are, but beneath the surface there is no distance at all. Physics tells us that a single electron cannot vibrate without making the whole universe shake. Every particle is part of a single field that stretches to infinity in all directions; this field feels and senses every single event instantly, no matter where it happens. As one witty physicist said, "If you tickle the universe over here, it laughs over there."

Imagine a small compass with its needle pointing north. It has no idea that a huge magnetic field is causing this, because the field is invisible. But if you move the compass, the field will pull the needle back in line without a pause. There's no need to send a signal to the magnetic North Pole and then receive one back. The field has sensed the compass and changed it; and in return the compass has changed the field, because no tiny part can shift without shifting the whole.

You are part of the cosmic field. Your body flows with magnetism, just like a compass, along with chemical and electrical energy. So your every thought is taking place not just in your head, but in the field. Your mind is eavesdropping on the universe.

Spirituality is a step ahead of science in one small way: It believes that the field is alive and intelligent. The whole universe *thinks*. There are some hints at this. Several years ago a colorful experiment was conducted using nonsense words. Children from Japan were shown a poem in Japanese and other words that formed nothing but nonsense. They could easily pick out which one was the poem. Then the same words were shown to Western kids who only spoke English. Strangely, they also showed an ability to pick out which words were a Japanese poem and which ones were nonsense. How did they do it? It was as if they picked this knowledge out of thin air—or as we would say, out of the field.

Does the field know Japanese? Maybe it knows a lot more. Albert Einstein himself said that when he plunged deep into the laws of nature, he was trying to figure out how God's mind worked, which is the same as saying that creation has a mind. I think it does, and so did Baba. Your intelligence is the same as cosmic intelligence. The eye keeps fooling you into thinking that the world is huge and you are small. But Baba never stopped trying to get me to stop believing my eyes.

There was once a great teacher who had many devoted followers. One day a young man came to him feeling very dejected and said, "You are so far above me that I can never rise that high. Lying in bed at night, I think of Jesus and Buddha and all the great masters. How can anyone as weak as me find enlightenment?"

The teacher thought for a moment and said, "You see yourself as small and weak because you look with physical eyes and not the eyes of the soul. I see the light in you, and

it is the same light that was in Jesus, Buddha, and all the
saints. Today it may be a small light, but its size doesn't
matter. Your light makes you one with the enlightened.
Just keep working until your full glory fills the world."

Out of My Way!

Baba was serious about taking me on a search. It was starting to feel like a safari. We trudged uphill and down without saying a word. I got the idea that he wanted me to think, so I ruminated until I got sick of that. "What are we doing?" I blurted out.

"What do you think we're doing?" he asked.

I wiped the sweat from my eyes and looked up at the blazing-hot, clear blue sky. "We're not looking for a rainbow, that's for sure."

"Don't get irritated," said Baba. "Let's look for something easier. How about God?"

"God?" That was a word Baba hardly ever used. "Why do you think God is easy to find? Most people think just the opposite," I said.

"That's because God has done such a good job of obeying us. Long ago people turned to God and said, 'Get out of our way, we know how to run the world,' and so he did. God's not getting in the way anymore."

"Baba, you're saying particularly strange things today," I said. "You think God left because we asked him to?"

"Without a doubt. I told you that you could change the world. God wouldn't have left the scene if that weren't true. He would have stayed around and run things himself."

"So he's really not here?"

"I didn't say that. It was almost impossible for him to find a way to leave. Then he came up with something clever. He vanished without vanishing." Instead of marching on, Baba came to a halt. He produced a small clay jar filled with water. He handed it to me and watched while I gulped it down.

"Don't you want any?" I asked.

"No, I want the jar empty." Baba took it from my hands. "Take a closer look. You see the clay walls of this jar? And you see the space inside?"

Suddenly he took a rock clenched in his other hand and smashed the jar to bits. "Have I smashed the space inside?" he asked.

"No."

"Now you see where God went. He may have erased the visible evidence that he was ever in this world, but he is just as present as the space inside this pot. Everywhere you look is a space for spirit. God is letting us make all the decisions because nothing we do can take his spirit away."

"Do people have to believe in God?" I asked.

"It's a choice," said Baba. "We all want to keep running our own lives, and some people feel better with God by their side, while others feel better thinking they are totally on their own. But that doesn't mean you made God disappear. He just disappeared *for you*. The divine plan could be working just fine, but you wouldn't know it."

WHAT I LEARNED

Baba was showing me something about who runs the world. If God is running it, he must be doing it with us or without us. If without us, then there's nothing for people to do, really, but worship the Almighty and hope to please him (or her). But if God is running the world *with* us, we need to step up and take our part seriously.

Baba believed that there is a divine plan, but God isn't showing us the blueprint, much less himself. So how are we meant to cooperate with his plan? Baba taught me that God is here in spirit. When I contact my spirit, I am helping the divine plan. Creation keeps going; it didn't happen just once. When I have a creative idea, God is having it through me. God's work is not like a final blueprint that no one is allowed to touch. "If you really want to see your maker," Baba said, "become a maker yourself. It's like catnip. God won't be able to resist helping you."

The more you stretch your mind into the unknown, the more help your soul will offer (this whole book is one long mind stretch, and I hope you will receive a flood of spiritual help from now on). I have learned to live by a piece of advice I read many years ago: "Start a great project, and with the first step you'll be amazed at the invisible forces that will come to your aid." What this means is that when you have a new thought, you are actually causing invisible forces to go on the alert; they notice you and try to help. Your choice is either to block them or to go with the flow. Here's what it takes to go with the flow.

A Game Plan for Accomplishment
1. Focus on what you want to accomplish, let it sprout and grow in your mind.
2. Ask your soul for help and encouragement.
3. Let go and allow the results to take shape.
4. Act when you feel clear.
5. Don't take any action when you're in doubt.
6. Don't spread confusion; have faith in your purpose.
7. Don't act on anger, anxiety, or other negative impulses.
8. Expect the best.
9. Accept every result as the best you can do at that moment.
10. Don't blame yourself for setbacks and obstacles.
11. Don't shrivel up and go tight inside when something

goes wrong. Be open to the lesson that every setback contains.

12. Don't blame others.

13. Know any outcome is possible.

14. Put the past behind you. Trust in a better future.

15. Don't accept bad outcomes passively—change whatever has to be changed within yourself.

16. Don't force or control the situation.

17. Don't go off in fantasy. Try to be as present as possible, without distraction.

18. Feel safe and centered inside.

19. Check all around you for signs that you are on the right path.

20. Be responsible for your own destiny.

The flow comes down to one thing: Spirit can accomplish anything once you get out of its way. When you are truly in the flow, there is much less struggle and stress. You don't have to try so hard.

Yet I mostly go back to this list when I'm *not* in the flow, when I need a reminder of all the blocks that make life difficult, such as negativity, criticism, losing trust, getting tense and tight inside, and so forth. These are just the *opposite* of what the list tells me to do. When you stop blocking yourself, you can get back to your calm and confident center. When you run into problems, turn them into spiritual lessons, such as learning to be patient and courageous. Nobody grows if everything comes too easily all the time. But you shouldn't consider struggle to be the normal or right way.

God is asking for cocreators, not soldiers. As spirit grows with you, you will find that being a creator is much easier and hugely more fun than winning any fight.

Pure Gold

Do you talk to God?" I asked Baba. "Does he talk to you?"

"In a way," he said. "I don't hear his voice, but I know what God wants anyway. That's the easiest thing in the world."

"Really?"

Baba had decided that we could rest for a while from our tramping. He found a stream deep in the woods, and we were dangling our feet in it to cool off.

"Nobody seems to think it's easy to figure out what God wants," I said. I wondered if Baba had another of his tricky answers up his sleeve.

"No tricks this time," he said. "Who could fool God? Although everyone tries to, all the time."

I thought he was going to launch off on that subject, but he gazed into the water for a long time. "This whole situation is muddy," he said. "So maybe you can tell me, what could God want if he's all-powerful—not to mention that he's not talking?"

"He could want a lot that I haven't figured out yet."

"Don't look so nervous," Baba said, smiling. "Maybe God isn't like a tough boss who demands more than you can give, even working overtime."

"That would be a relief," I admitted. "But I'd rather hear what you were going to tell me."

"God can want only one thing," said Baba, who then told me the following story:

One day in a rich man's house nobody was home, and all his expensive things started an argument.

"I'm the most precious thing here," a gold ring declared proudly.

"No, you're not," a gold necklace said even more haughtily. "Look how complicated and beautiful I am. No simple little ring can compare with me."

"You're both wrong," said a gold watch with disdain. "I'm ten times more complicated than any necklace, and besides that, I'm useful, too."

The argument only got worse, until a grandfather clock in the corner broke in. "You're all wrong," he said. "A ring isn't the same as a necklace, and a necklace isn't the same as a watch. But you are all made of the same pure gold, and that makes you equal."

Baba looked at me when he finished his tale. "Do you see what it's about?" he asked. "God is like the grandfather clock, who sees everyone as spirit, but we go around seeing differences. We think that what we look like, what we say and do, determines who we are. That's why God wants only one thing: He wants us to drop our disguises. Once you see yourself as he sees you, there is nothing more that God could ever want."

WHAT I LEARNED

This lesson made me breathe a sigh of relief. I used to worry a lot about what God wanted me to do, and even more about what he might do to me if he got angry. It seemed incredibly difficult to figure out. Being "holy" and yet a normal kid at the same time didn't seem possible. But Baba taught me that being spiritual has nothing to do with pretending you're holy or trying to imitate someone you think is holy. You are spiritual when you stop pretending that God is anywhere but in you. That's what Baba's parable was about. The pure gold in the story is the most valuable thing on Earth, and so is spirit. The only thing that comes close is air, which you can't put a price on, even though it sustains all life.

I have heard people say that human beings are angels in disguise. Each of us has been given a mission here on Earth, but after we get our orders, God erases the memory at birth so that we can have the adventure of finding out on our own what we're meant to do down here. I like that idea, but a person can have a divine mission without being an angel. The following story may strike close to home:

When God created the world he summoned his angels and said, "I am making human beings in my image. They will be creative, intelligent, and good. Everything divine will be theirs by birthright."

The angels said, "But if they know the truth about themselves, their lives will be too smooth and boring."

"Then I'll hide the truth on the highest mountaintop," said God.

"Human beings can easily figure out how to climb the highest mountain," the angels said.

"Then I'll sink it in the deepest ocean," said God.

"Human beings will figure out how to dive into the deepest ocean," the angels said.

The discussion raged about where the truth could be hidden from such clever creatures. In the clouds? On the moon? Among the distant galaxies? Then God had a brilliant idea. "I know," he said. "I'll put the truth in the human heart. That's the last place they will ever look." The angels applauded, and that's exactly what he did.

The story is funny and sad at the same time. As long as people keep wearing disguises, the truth will remain well hidden in their hearts. In a way Baba's lesson was strange, because if you think about it, the creator of the universe couldn't really want anything. God is already everywhere. He's not an old man sitting on a throne in the sky. God isn't even a he or a she. God is spirit itself. But if you imagine him as a human being, God would want us to appreciate one truly amazing fact: Our essence and his are exactly the same. Spirit is spirit, whether you find it in a human being or in the creator. Go ahead, take a closer look—the resemblance is unmistakable.

The Sweet Life

I must have dozed off beside the stream, because the next thing I could feel was warm grass under my cheek. I sat up, rubbing my eyes. "Are we ready to go?" I mumbled.

"We don't have to," said Baba. "I found what I was looking for." It took a second for me to realize that he was staring at the sky, and when I looked up, it was there. A rainbow.

"But that's impossible," I exclaimed. The sky was as clear as before, but there was no denying that a perfect arc of a rainbow was hanging over us. I felt the grass all around me. "The ground's dry. What's happening?"

"I can give you two explanations," Baba said quickly. He wanted to head off any idea that he had performed some kind of magic trick. "Sometimes rainbows can appear in a clear blue sky because moisture is trapped in the air. The moisture forms tiny droplets that bend the light just right. It's rare, but it happens."

"What's the second explanation?" I asked, thinking that the first was good enough.

"A rainbow appeared because we were looking for one."

I said, "That explanation is a lot harder to believe."

Baba shrugged. "Then why not pick both?"

"Because only one can be right," I said.

"If you learn to see beyond the surface, both can be right. Moisture had to form that rainbow. But my soul also knew that I was looking for one." Baba sounded too certain for me to argue with, and I was beginning to believe him, as I did on so many occasions when he said something impossible.

He went on. "I told you that God doesn't seem to be around, but he is doing what we want anyway. Spirit's assignment is to turn our thoughts into reality. And God never leaves anyone out. Looking at a rainbow, some will see water droplets bending light, others will see a moment of delight provided by spirit."

We lay back now and watched the rainbow, which was getting brighter by the moment. Somehow seeing it without clouds was eerie but just as glorious. "Why does a rainbow make me feel so good?" I asked.

"Because life is meant to be sweet, and when you see something as sweet as a rainbow, it makes you remember that." Baba said nothing more as the rainbow faded, leaving behind no trace that it had ever existed.

WHAT I LEARNED

That rainbow has followed me a long time. When I grew up I got almost all my college training in science, so my mind learned the kinds of explanations that leave out the soul. But Baba taught me that moments of delight, the times when life is truly sweet, come from spirit. I had to teach myself to look under the surface and find the hidden taste of sweetness. If a rainbow can be hiding in a clear blue sky, then who knows what else is hiding inside an ordinary day?

People ask, "How do you define God?" Baba had the simplest answer I've ever heard: He's the surprise you never expected. He's the rainbow in a clear blue sky. That's a colorful way of saying that God is the spirit that amazes us in ordinary things. God is not as distant as people seem to think. To find him, you only have to get closer a day at a time. Going about your old routine won't do it, though. You must step out of the ordinary. Otherwise, where's the surprise?

Better than any rainbow is to surprise yourself. Beneath the surface every day presents at least one chance for a spiritual surprise. You are very different beneath the surface than anyone ever thought. I came up with an A-to-Z list to create moments of "Aha!" every day. Pick any letter at random, and under that letter will be a simple way to see yourself as you never have before—as someone who has the same power and vision as your soul.

A
Soul Alphabet

APPRECIATION

Today, decide to appreciate somebody. Appreciation shouldn't be silent. It's the best way to show that you don't take anyone for granted. I can remember words people told me years and years ago that changed how I saw myself. "You are a good person" is an incredibly powerful statement from the right person, someone you really respect. "You're so thoughtful" or "I like the way you say things" or "I'm glad I can count on you" are all words of appreciation that someone you know wants to hear. When people sell a house and get more than they expected for it, they say it appreciated in value. The same is true for human beings. If you appreciate them, they will increase in value before your very eyes.

BEYOND

Today, decide that you will look beyond your own point of view. Say to someone, "Tell me more about how you see things." It's easy to find a time to do that—just wait until you think you have the most important thing to say, then stop and let someone else speak instead. The soul takes in all points of view, and the more you imitate that habit, the more spiritual your life will become. Baba had a good way of explaining this.

"Do you know the story of the blind men and the elephant?" he asked.

I did. In India every child is told the fable about how six wise men tried to describe an elephant, but each was blind. The first blind man felt the elephant's side and said, "I know what an elephant is, it's very much like a wall." The second blind man felt the elephant's tusk and said, "No, an elephant is very much like a spear." The third blind man took hold of the trunk, so to him an elephant was much like a snake. And so it went. The tail felt like a rope, the ear like a fan, the leg like a tree. None of them got it completely right, so there's a moral: If you know only a little bit about something, you don't really know it at all.

"That still leaves a riddle, though," said Baba. "Why do you suppose they picked the number six? Why not seven blind men or three? Six stands for the five senses and the mind. We use these six things to figure out what the universe is like. For the universe is the elephant, and the real moral of the tale is that you cannot trust your senses to tell you what is real, no matter how hard you think about it. It takes something else—the eye of the soul—to truly see the elephant."

COMMUNICATE

Today, tell someone about a feeling you've been keeping to yourself. Be brave enough to communicate. Communicating has two sides. There's what you say and there's what you don't say. Most spiritual feelings fall into the second category. It's hard to talk about feeling that God loves you, or the opposite, that he doesn't love you. It's hard to talk about your deepest feelings for your family. But spirit doesn't like to be trapped inside, so don't keep these feelings private forever, or they will become stuck.

You don't have to start with something really deep and personal. Find someone today who will listen to just one feeling you haven't expressed before. It could be as simple as "I think we're a lot alike, but I never told you" or "I feel really comfortable around you." As a start this may sound pretty basic, but this is a powerful way to reach your soul. Revealing what's in your soul is like using the telephone. You can't expect to reach anyone if the line is cut. People think they're being put on hold when they call God, but actually the line is out. "Why doesn't God just repair the line himself?" I asked Baba.

"Because he's not the one who cut it," Baba said. "If you begin right now to communicate what's really in your heart, you will be repairing the line, bit by bit, until you and spirit are on speaking terms once again."

DOING FOR OTHERS

Today, decide to do something for others. Pick an action that you'd like someone to do for you. At home this can be as simple as bringing food to the dinner table without being asked or making the bed for someone (they'll probably faint, so this is an especially good choice). Or you could save a place in line at the movies for someone who's not already your friend.

Whatever you choose, do it in the spirit of unselfishness. How do you know what that feels like? Baba had a surprising idea about that. "When you do anything for another person, it must feel as if you are doing it for yourself."

"That sounds strange," I said.

"But true. At the soul level there is no difference between you and another person. The feeling you get from helping them is just as sweet as if you did the same deed for yourself. Sweeter, in fact, because every unselfish act allows more love to come into this world. What could be better than that?"

EXPAND

Today, decide to expand the way you see. Explore a book—maybe on astronomy or medicine—that everyone else would think is too difficult for you. If you go to a football game, try rooting for both sides. If you are a boy, spend five minutes thinking about how a girl would see a certain situation, or reverse that if you are a girl. Seeing things as the opposite sex does is always expansive because we spend so much time believing that the man's way or the woman's way has to be right. Baba took this much further. He thought everyone should expand on five levels every day.

Mind: You are expanding mentally if you understand more about life and the soul.

Body: You are expanding physically if you feel light, carefree, and safe in the world.

Emotions: You are expanding emotionally if you feel happier and more positive. At the same time fear and anger don't cloud you with their negativity.

Psychology: You are expanding psychologically if you feel more free.

Spirit: You are expanding spiritually when your vision of life is coming true.

I apply these five levels to myself, and only if I am expanding on all of them do I feel I'm really getting closer to my soul.

FORGIVENESS

Today, forgive somebody for one thing that hurt you in the past. You don't have to talk to the person who wronged you or make an announcement. But you do have to truly forgive, which means that from this day on the wrong has been erased completely. You will treat that person as if the hurt never happened. (I'm sure you've met people who say "I forgive you" on Monday but somehow manage to dredge up your offenses on Tuesday—or the next time they get irritated. If you find yourself saying, "Remember that time you did X to me?" then you haven't really forgiven or forgotten.)

Even if somebody in your life needs a lot of forgiving, you can find one small thing to start with. Baba knew that even this was a challenge, however.

"Do you find it hard to forgive people who've done something wrong?" he asked me.

"Sure, especially if they did it to me," I said.

"Then why bother to try?" he asked.

"Because you're supposed to."

"Ah, now you know why *not* to forgive," Baba said. "Anything you do because you are supposed to is forced.

Remember the times as a child when you were told to make up with your brother after a fight? The only reason you did was because your parents were standing over you. That kind of forgiveness only creates more resentment, which you will bury because resentment is supposed to be bad. There is another way. Forgive because it makes you feel better. Forgive because it removes toxic memories from your mind. Forgive because it opens the door for accepting yourself. In the end you cannot accept yourself without forgiveness, because in your heart of hearts you know that you want to be forgiven too. Once you admit that to yourself, people will hear the sincerity in your voice when you forgive them."

GIFT

Today, decide that you will look upon life as a gift. Take a moment to list the blessings in your life. Maybe that sounds corny, but Baba found it very important.

"Do you think every day is a gift?" he asked me.

"Well . . ."

"I thought so. The funny thing is that people mostly want to grab at life. They want more and more for themselves. With that attitude life isn't a gift, it's more like loot that you are robbing from someone," Baba said. "To make every day feel like a gift, you must feel deep down that no one can take it from you. Isn't that what a gift is— something completely yours without strings attached? Life seems to have strings attached. You must work and prove yourself; you must strive for love and approval that may be taken away.

"All these things exist in the mind, however. To your soul, life is purely a gift. It is ever fresh, ever flowing, like water in a fountain. This attitude is also the key to giving. When you can truly say to yourself, 'Everything I have came from God and goes back to God,' then you can give to others in the same spirit that life was given to you."

HEART AWARENESS

Today, decide to see the world with your heart and not your head. To imagine what that's like, think about how a mother feels toward her child. No matter how many ways the child may decide to be bad, its mother doesn't change her love. She sees her child with heart awareness. You can do that for anyone you happen to pick. Overlook their faults for just ten minutes, seeing them as totally good. Baba was very clear that we all need to practice this because we use our minds far too much.

"Your head isn't shy about ruling your heart. It will remind you every day why you should look down on person A, resent person B, never forgive person C. It will show you faults and imperfections everywhere you look. The heart doesn't do that. It asks one simple question: *Am I feeling love?* If the answer is yes, then you have true heart awareness. If the answer is no, you must get back to heart awareness. Most of spiritual life comes down to letting love have its rightful place at the center of life."

INSPIRATION

Today, let something inspire you. Allow yourself a moment when you go, "Aha!" If possible, look at a work of genius, like a great painting, or listen to music that takes your breath away. Baba put a high value on inspiration because he traced it back to the soul.

"Inspiration shouldn't be mechanical; it's not like throwing a switch," he said. "Your soul knows when you need to be inspired. The word itself means 'bringing in spirit.' When do you need to bring in spirit? Who can say? It might be five seconds from now, it might be this evening when you see the sunset or tomorrow when your eye is charmed by a baby in the park.

"But always know this: Inspiration isn't optional. Your soul uses it to get through, to send you a message. That sunset is about you, and so is that baby in the park. Inspiration isn't reserved only for great deeds and great works of art. Be attentive, appreciate your life and all who are in it, set yourself a vision. With these things in place the door to inspiration is always open."

JUSTICE

Today, be fair to somebody who needs it. Justice is fairness, and the opposite of justice is unfairness in all its forms. Unjust treatment turns people into victims, and that is not what the soul wants. It's fair to be told the truth. It's fair to be seen as equal. It's fair to share in the good things of this world.

If you know someone who is on the wrong end of fairness, do something to make it right. Share your time, money, food, or simply your respect with someone who lacks these things. You'll be doing exactly what you think God should do for you.

Baba once asked me, "Have you heard people say that life is unfair?"

"All the time," I said.

"But they also say that God is just. So which is it? Some spiritual questions make a huge difference, and this is one. Either life is unfair or God is just."

"I guess people *hope* that God is just, but no one can prove it. Anyone can see that life isn't fair," I said.

"I can't," said Baba. "Nobody ever handed me a set of rules. For all I know, God may be handing out cosmic justice, but I don't have cosmic eyes; therefore, I will never know. But I do know one thing: Sometimes life says yes to me, and sometimes life says no. If you really look at it, most people think life is unfair because they hit a no when they wanted a yes.

"If you could get life to say yes more often, you'd think there was justice in the universe. Wanting a yes is natural. It's the very thing your soul is trying to achieve. I've shown you many ways to live from the level of the soul. Once you do that, life will begin to feel much more fair."

"But I will still see terrible things happening to other people," I said.

"Everything you see in the world reflects the power for good and evil that is inside you," said Baba. "Solve the question of whether life is fair. Go as deep as you can. Never stop asking what the divine plan is. You'll never find a complete answer, but layer by layer you will come to see that God did not create an unjust world. He created a world where all possibilities, including triumph and tragedy, play themselves out, exactly as they do in our hearts."

KINDNESS

Today, take a moment to show some kindness. Treat someone better than you are used to; understand the feelings of someone who has been hurt; spend time with a sick patient or a loner at school who is dying for a kind word and rarely gets one. Baba knew that kindness can be difficult, even with people we love.

"Have you ever been mean to your little brother?" he asked me.

"He thinks so," I replied, hoping to dodge the question.

"It's strange how mean we can be to our own kind," he said. "Did you ever notice that *kind* has this second meaning? Those who are most like you, your people, are called your kind.

"Let's say you didn't have a little brother, but a twin instead, and let's say your twin was so perfect that he did everything you do. Would you always be kind to him?" asked Baba.

"We'd still fight sometimes," I said.

"Yes, the closer people are, the more flaws they see in one another," Baba said. "But if you can't be kind to your perfect twin, then why be kind to anybody?"

"Because you just feel like it," I said.

"Feelings are tricky. They tend to turn bad when you aren't looking," said Baba. "Your soul has a better reason. Stop looking for flaws, and kindness comes much more easily. You always have that choice. We spend a lot of time overlooking our own faults. Spend a fraction of that time overlooking the faults of someone else, and soon you will see that other people deserve the same kindness you want them to show to you. The minute you see that kindness is *deserved,* you will not be casually mean to anyone again."

LOVE AND LIKE

Today, take time to like someone you already love. Does this sound strange? Most of the people we love are in our family. Loving them is part of being there, while liking them is another matter. Baba talked to me about this.

"Why do I hear people say, 'I love you, but I don't like you'?" he asked.

"I don't know. It feels peculiar when someone says that," I replied.

"Because they are sending two messages at once," said Baba. "'I love you, but you have done bad things to me.' It's very hard to like someone who doesn't do what pleases you. If a friend makes you jealous or resentful, like goes out the window."

"Until you get over it," I said.

"Your soul knows a different way," said Baba. "There is a place inside you that has never been hurt and never will be. If you lie in bed, sometimes you can feel it as a softness in your heart, a warm sense of belonging that nobody can take away from you. You don't have to struggle to find that feeling; you only have to uncover it. Once you do, love and like will stop being such a problem, because you won't need your friends to act just the way you want before you can like them. And those you love will be likable because you have stopped saying, 'I like you only when you're nice to me.'"

MUSIC OF NATURE

Today, go outside and discover the music of nature. Some people say that after God created the world, he felt like signing his work, as a painter signs a painting. So he left behind two things to remind us of heaven: waterfalls and rainbows. I like that idea, but Baba took it even further.

"Did you know that there's a kind of music you can see?" asked Baba. I shook my head. "It's the music of nature. Go outside sometime and try to see it."

"How?"

"Begin by letting a beautiful sound reach your ears, such as the singing of birds or the rush of a stream," Baba said. "Now open your eyes and take in the scene. Don't focus on the sound or the sight you see, let them blend. Imagine your vision getting bigger and bigger as you take in the trees, the clouds, the sky. It all hangs together, just as a perfect day seems to hang together. That harmony is the music of nature. It isn't any one thing, no matter how beautiful. It is the beauty of One. If the angels really play music for God, this is what they play, an eternal song in praise of unity."

NEGATIVITY

Today, avoid the temptation to be negative. It's negative to criticize, to blame somebody else, to demand perfection, to treat someone as inferior or not your kind of person. How many times have you heard somebody justify these behaviors? Perform an experiment for one day. See how you feel after not being critical, not blaming anyone, not seeing anybody else as inferior. You'll find a lot of surprises, such as how often people are negative without thinking they are, and how good it feels to go one day without putting a single person down in any way.

"All negativity is based on the word *no*," Baba told me. "When you say no, you keep life from flowing where it wants to go. Your no blocks the flow."

"Sometimes you have to say no," I pointed out.

"We're not talking about saying no when you see something wrong," he said. "If a baby gets too close to the fire, then no is a way to protect it from harm. But for every time that kind of situation comes up, people say a hundred noes that could be yeses. There is a deeper mystery here than they realize.

"Life is always positive. Its power is used to create

growth. So if you say yes, you harness the power of growth, while saying no makes things shrink away and stop growing."

I shook my head. "I still don't see how you can always say yes."

"Words are secondary," replied Baba. "It comes down to allowing. Either you allow life to unfold or you don't. When you try to force anyone to do something, when you manipulate or control, beg or whine, those are signs that you don't trust life to unfold. You want to step in on your own. Any time you feel totally alone fighting for yourself, some kind of negativity is at work. Yet your soul would never leave you alone; it always offers the support of life with all its infinite power.

"Learning to allow takes time. Be on the alert when you are tempted to say no. Ask yourself, 'Can this situation work out if I just allow?' The more you allow spirit to solve problems, the closer you will come to harnessing the power that lies at the very heart of life."

OPEN

Today, be open to a new possibility. It's easy to close your mind and harder to open it. But your soul wants you to be more open every day.

"God is always ready to be surprised," said Baba. "When he created the world, the first thing he said was, 'Let's hope it works.'"

"That's a joke, right?" I said.

"It could also be wisdom," said Baba. "Water can't flow through a pipe unless it's open, and you are the pipe that life flows through. If you want more out of life, just be more open—open to new ideas and experiences, open to what others think, open to the unknown that is just around the corner. Some people are proud of knowing what they know. They shouldn't be. The more you *don't* know, the more you see the mystery that's all around you."

Being open scares some people, so they try to keep everything under control. But when you are open, life really gets much sweeter. You allow things to happen, you let other people be themselves. "I want to be me" is a desire everyone has in their heart. Today you can help someone be themselves with the following steps:

Be relaxed in your attitude. Show that you are friendly and approachable. Even if you are used to the way boys challenge one another and act aggressive to show that they are part of the gang, give that behavior a rest.

Give your competitive streak a rest too. Instead of competing, find a quiet place to talk about what's happening in your life.

Listen. Turn off the TV and computer. Get the other person to open up, then focus on what they want to say. When you listen, you immediately bring other people on your side. Test it out for yourself: When someone quietly listens to you, don't you feel accepted? Today you can give that same feeling to someone else.

Share a secret. Nothing is better at showing that you feel trusting and open.

Be honest but not critical. Openness means you don't hold back, you say what is really in your heart. But being negative makes others tense, and today that's the opposite of what you want.

These are simple steps, but there's a kind of magic in them. Without saying a word, by simply being open, you can have a totally new relationship with your family, for example. You will instantly be perceived as no longer a threat to anyone. And these steps aren't just for now. They will serve you well for the rest of your life.

PARENTS

Today, imagine that you are a parent. Pick a friend and look at him or her, not with today in mind, but the years ahead. What kind of future would you tell your friend to work toward? Listen to what your friend is saying and ask yourself, "What kind of child did I raise?" Do you hear the values you hoped would be there? Put yourself in the shoes of someone who has to worry about where your friend goes at night and who he or she hangs out with. Parenting isn't a job, but a state of mind. If you can begin to see one other person like a parent does, you will get a hint of God's point of view.

"Who would you rather have for a father?" asked Baba. "Your own dad or God?"

"That's easy. I'd choose my dad," I said.

"Why?"

"God knows everything you do. He sees every bad thought. There's not a lot of wiggle room."

"But isn't God supposed to be perfect?" asked Baba, smiling. "Why would you need wiggle room?"

"Perfect creates a lot of stress. I don't think I could breathe around God," I said.

"Fair enough. Parents are worried about being perfect too. They are trying to be as fair as love can be. But in truth God is doing that as well. Your soul doesn't push. It knows where you are sensitive or self-conscious, and it allows you to keep your secrets for as long as you want.

"If you see things this way, it becomes a lot easier to understand why parents are the way they are. They fit into what your own soul wants you to hear. Begin to appreciate your parents from the spiritual level whenever you are tempted to do battle. See them as two souls working in cooperation with your soul. Then one day you will see that you also taught them many things. Every child is also a parent at the soul level."

QUESTIONING

Today, do two things that may sound like opposites: Ask yourself a new question and answer an old one. The new question is easy to find. Pick up any book about human nature, maybe a novel or a book on psychology or relationships. Find a part of the story where two people are in conflict, perhaps a couple who are fighting. Ask yourself, "If I had to decide this argument, which side would I pick?" Then pick the other side and ask why it is right instead. Questioning keeps your mind sharp and focused.

But the mind also needs to settle on answers. So take a question that nobody seems to know the answer to: Is there a God? Does Satan exist? What happens after we die? Give yourself an answer and watch what happens. The instant you answer a question, many new possibilities come to mind. It's a sort of reverse psychology, because the instant you are sure you know something, a little voice inside can't help but chime in with, *Maybe, but what about X?* Baba taught me to respect both sides of questioning.

"People say you should never stop asking questions, but I only half believe that," he said. "You should also keep accepting answers."

"I don't see how they can go together," I said.

"They can, once you see that questions aren't meant to last forever. If someone spends a lifetime looking for God without finding him, that would be a terrible waste."

"It happens all the time," I pointed out.

"The problem is doubt," said Baba. "Doubt doesn't lead to answers; it only breeds more doubt. Many people would like to know that God is real, but they aren't willing to give up their doubts along the way. They would rather keep them intact until God gives them a sign."

"How do you get around that?" I asked. "I mean, their doubt is real."

"Let one answer unfold at a time," said Baba. "When you make a best friend, he doesn't have to prove himself all over again every time you meet. Yet you make God go back to zero when anything goes wrong.

"Be more accepting. When you see a reason to think that life is good, believe in that reason and don't go back on it. The next reason will be more convincing. Going back to doubt every time is what turns life into one big question. Keep your eye on the answers. They are coming your way all the time, in small hints and clues."

I've tried to live that way, but one small worry keeps returning, so I'll bring it up here. I've met hundreds of people who don't believe in a personal God. Some tell me that they believe in a higher self. Some use the word *spirit*, and they pray to the universe the way other people pray to

God. All of them, however, feel a higher purpose. They aren't willing to settle for a world without spirit.

So I stopped saying, "I am looking for God." I don't often hear myself saying, "I believe in God," or even, "There is a God." To really know the truth about love or faith or the soul itself, trust in small answers first. Let them grow instead of being smothered at birth by your doubts. Then an amazing thing can happen. You can wake up one morning to discover that everything God stands for is true. God is real by any name you use, or none at all.

RESPOND

Today, give somebody a response instead of a reaction. There is a big difference between the two: Reactions come automatically, responses take a bit of thought. Most of the time you can handle life using nothing but reactions. Want salad or a hamburger for lunch? *Hamburger.* Got time for a video game? *Sure.* When are you going to do your homework? *Later.* A reaction is like putting a penny in the slot and getting the answer automatically.

Each of these questions could have led to a response instead. Want salad or a hamburger for lunch? *What kind of salad were you thinking of?* Got time for a video game? *Isn't there something new we could do?* When are you going to do your homework? *As soon as I have quiet time when I can think.* Notice the difference? The responses aren't mechanical like reactions, and they don't just pop out automatically.

Starting today, get into the habit of responding. It doesn't take more effort—you simply pause and wait to see if a new response wants to come up. You'll get the reaction first because it pops up without thinking. But there will be something new if you wait and give yourself room to think. The deepest responses come from the soul. A spiritual life never comes automatically, so by pausing to see what is really inside you, you are making a connection to spirit, with all its invisible gifts.

SEEING

Today, practice the art of seeing. Anybody can see, but to *really see* is an art. I'm sure you see a flower every day. But with the art of seeing, here's how a daisy looks: It has a swirling yellow center, like a pinwheel. That same swirl appears in the shell of a chambered nautilus deep in the sea. It shows up in the swirl of DNA in all your cells, and also in the swirl of stars billions of light-years away in distant galaxies. So if you really see a daisy, you see from here to infinity, from the smallest speck of matter to the vast reach of outer space.

"I have taught you a new way of seeing," Baba told me. "But really it's an eternal way of seeing. In every speck of creation there is the entire history of the universe. And beyond each speck is the pure place that holds essence, which is the real you."

Seeing is an art when you can start anywhere and wind up with spirit. That is what it means to see with the eye of the soul.

THAT

Today, go on a hunt for the legendary creature known as That. It has no proper name, and yet people are sure they've seen it. That is the flash of joy in the eyes of someone you love. That is in the way your heart soars over the open water out at sea. That is the thrill of being on a mountaintop or dreaming that you can fly or lying in a meadow and knowing, for a split second, that you can touch a cloud.

But That is tricky because it doesn't stay around for long and is always on the move. Every time you think you've caught up with it, you find that it left five minutes ago. Even so, people never stop looking for That. Once in its presence, you never forget it. Which is why some people claim that That must be God.

UNITY

Today, take a step closer to unity. Unity is when you no longer see differences, but feel completely one with everything. To be one with yourself is the goal of life. But today you only need to take a small step in that direction. How? By quitting the game of us versus them. We all know that game; it pits one side against the other for no reason except to look better.

"Everyone wants to feel special," said Baba. "That's why it's so tempting to claim you're better than somebody else because you're older or smarter, or you hang out with better friends, or you can put on a good show of attitude.

"But this game doesn't really make anyone happy. You'll always be afraid that the tables might be turned. What do you do when 'them' is the side that gets the power or becomes superior? What do you do when us versus them stops being a game and leads to war?"

The game of us versus them starts fairly innocently. You begin to compare yourself. *Are my clothes as nice as hers? Can I lift as much weight as him? Did I get a C- when my friend got a B+?* You feel resentful to be on the low side of the comparison, yet being on the high side brings no peace either, because there's no such thing as being better all the time. So this is a great game to give up—you win by walking away.

"If you want to be in the joy of unity," said Baba, "stop comparing yourself with everybody. The game of us versus them only makes differences worse. At the level of spirit there's a secret people don't like to see: Us and them are the same. As soon as you see that, fear of losing goes away. The grand prize in us versus them is that somebody gets to feel special for a while. The grand prize in the game of unity is that everyone gets to feel special forever."

VOICE OF SILENCE

Today, listen to the voice of silence. You already know how to listen to all kinds of voices (and how to block them out). This voice is different, because it's the closest thing anyone can hear of God's voice. Spirit doesn't need words. It can help you in other ways:

Spirit can make you certain that you know something. This is called intuition.

Spirit can settle the mind into quietness. This is called peace.

Spirit can keep you from being stressed and overwhelmed by the chaos around you. This is called detachment.

Spirit can remove self-doubt. This is called being centered.

All these gifts are brought to you by the voice of silence. You can't work for them, run after them, think them into existence, or make them up. The key is to relax, go inside, and make friends with the silence. Use some time today to do that. Everyone's mind is very active and noisy, so you'll notice those things at first. But that's just on the surface. Deeper down the mind likes being quiet. Think about how soothing those moments are just before you fall asleep or just after you wake up in the morning. The voice of silence speaks clearly in those moments, and you can ask it to speak anytime you want. In time it will become the voice you trust more than anyone else's.

WEALTH

Today, make yourself wealthy. In one day you can't give yourself a pile of money, but that isn't the secret of wealth. As long as you can tap into the flow of nature's abundance, you will be wealthy, not tomorrow or next year, but at this moment. Your wealth will come as new life, new ideas, new reasons to be joyful, new ways to fulfill your desires. God's plan is always for more wealth and never for lack.

If you ever feel you are lacking, look around. Nature is lavishly abundant everywhere you look—in every seed is the promise of a whole forest, in the fertilized egg inside a mother's womb is the promise of the billions of cells in your body today. This abundance started flowing from the first instant of the big bang and has never stopped. Creation is now, and so is wealth.

"I am wealthy," Baba told me. "In fact, I'm the wealthiest person I've ever met."

I had to laugh. "Baba, you don't have a cent. You get to eat because someone invites you in every night. You wear the same clothes until they are worn out. I don't think you even have money."

"But somehow the universe has met every need I've

ever had," said Baba. "You will be the wealthiest man in the world if you have enough money to do what you need to do *right now*."

I wondered if I would ever be brave enough to test out Baba's theory. I've tested it enough to know that spirit doesn't see any difference between a penny and a billion dollars. It gives according to the need that must be filled. Having your needs met should be as simple as holding a bucket under a flowing faucet. But the flow is blocked by fear, contraction, self-doubt, and confusion. Every time you remove the smallest bit of blockage, spirit's abundance will flow a little more.

The most important thing is not to cling to money as if you have found true wealth. A person who hoards money is saying, "I don't trust the flow of abundance. There is only limited wealth, and I must grab mine first." Wouldn't you rather be someone who says, "I see a need that I can fulfill. I trust that everything will come to me from the source"? God's mind is infinitely rich with ideas, and each idea takes shape. Right now you are taking shape in his mind, and whatever you need will come about as you grow.

X FACTOR

Today, give in to the X factor, which is the unknown. Many people are afraid of the unknown. They eat the same food today as yesterday, hang out with the same friends, watch the same shows, and play the same games. Inside they are also thinking the same thoughts—a psychologist once estimated that if you took every thought you had today, 90 percent would be thoughts you had yesterday.

Creation would be incredibly boring if nature did that. So the X factor was built into creation. It's the creative factor, something you can't predict.

"Would you like an exciting life?" Baba asked me.

"Of course."

"Then here's how to get one," he said. "When you wake up tomorrow, say to your soul, 'Make today unpredictable.' Once you've said this prayer, forget about it; allow spirit to bring you something you never expected."

I followed his advice (and taught my own children this prayer) because any time things don't go the way I planned, I can say to myself, "God heard my prayer, all right. He gave me something I would never have predicted."

There's no better way to get over your fear of the unknown. The *X* factor is the most creative force in the universe. You'll never know what's coming next, but you can be certain that a surprise is on its way.

You

Today, make some time for the real you. The other you is used to getting so much attention that it never stops asking for more. But the real you has asked for nothing. It's the you that is quiet, happy to be itself, needing no one, afraid of nothing. The reason it doesn't speak up for itself is that it has a lot of patience. The real you is who you want to be once you try out all the other models, the ones other people want you to be.

Which reminds me of an old fable. A man was walking down the road with his wife, their little boy, and a donkey. Seeing them, some onlookers said, "Bad man! You own a donkey, but you make your poor family walk?"

So the man put his son on the donkey and went a little farther. Seeing them, some onlookers said, "Foolish man! You own a sturdy donkey, and all you put on it is a little boy?"

So the man put his wife on the donkey too and went a little farther. Seeing them, some onlookers said, "You weakling! You let your wife order a ride while you have to walk?"

So all three got on the donkey, which staggered home, and soon after, it died of exhaustion.

The moral of the tale is, don't live for the approval of others. The real you is here to find out the secret of life, not to satisfy someone else's opinion. Sit quietly today, close your eyes, and begin to make the acquaintance of this inner friend who will never desert you.

ZERO

Today, hold a celebration over nothing. Put a candle in a piece of cake, have an extra scoop of ice cream. You are giving thanks for zero, or nothing, because nothing is where all invisible things come from.

"Zero has always been a number for God," Baba said. "Because if you add zero to zero, you get zero. If you multiply zero by zero, divide zero by zero, or even add an infinite number of zeros to the first zero, the answer is always zero. So it is with God. You cannot add, subtract, multiply, or divide God without the sum total being God."

Whenever you think that you are facing a zero chance, realize that you are actually facing an infinite chance. Zero isn't an end point, but a starting point. It's the empty void that gave birth to the whole universe. And if the day comes when you feel so blue that you are tempted to say, "I'm nothing," stop and realize this: You are right to see yourself as "no thing," because you are spirit. If you are "no thing," that puts you close to God, and if you have nothing, you have infinite possibilities waiting to be born.

The Last Word

The fourth day that I was with Baba turned out to be my last. He didn't tell me my soul training was over. We both knew that it had just begun. But he did have one last grand flourish up his sleeve.

We were sitting under the old, twisted tree. The sun was low and the light golden. Baba had fixed his eyes on a sunbeam that filtered down through the tree's thick canopy.

"Why are you staring?" I asked.

"I want to see if I've done my job well."

It was the last mysterious thing he would ever say to me, and like all the rest, it made me curious. I stared at the sunbeam too. There was nothing special about it. If I looked close, I could see dancing motes of dust in the light.

But as I kept looking something changed. The light began to shimmer. It was tossing the dust motes around as if they were dancing together. Suddenly I knew something

I didn't know before: Light is *alive*. I kept staring, and for the first time I didn't see light—I saw into it, into its secret life.

"It looks happy," I said, because I couldn't find any other word.

"Not just happy," said Baba. "Joyful. Every speck of creation feels like that. There are worlds in every mote of dust, and this world you live in is another mote of dust among millions that burst into creation."

He was right. The closer I looked, the more it seemed as if the whole world could be a speck of dust set dancing by God. The sunbeam quivered faster and brighter, glowing with joy.

How did I ever miss this?

"Just so you don't miss it again," said Baba, reading my mind, "be sure to remember this moment." He stood up as the sunbeam faded away. "I haven't done too badly if you can see what you've seen today. And don't worry, you'll see a lot more."

That was his good-bye, I suppose. He started walking toward the road. I followed, and as we reached the overlook where the valley was spread out, I kept telling myself that Baba would be back tomorrow.

"There's no tomorrow," he said, pausing to drink in the view. "Time is a toy I threw away a long time ago." He gave me one last look, with his head cocked to the side like a curious parrot. Then the old man walked away for good. I believe him when he said that he threw time away, because even though I've never set eyes on Baba since I was fifteen years old, not a day goes by but he is with me—he's an extension of my own self.